SO I HAVE THIS THEORY...

SO, I HAVE THIS THEORY...

**A COMEDY
BY CALEB ZWAR**

Copyright © 2011 by Caleb Zwar

All rights reserved. No part of this book may be reproduced in whole or in part, or stored in a retrieval system, or transmitted in any form or by any means, electronic, mechanical, photocopying, recording, or otherwise, without written permission by the publisher.
ISBN: 1-257-77505-7

A huge thanks to my friends and family,
who listened to these crazy ideas over the years,
especially my ever-patient and loving wife!

So I Have This Theory...

CONTENTS

Foreword	6
Introduction	10
Migration Patterns	16
Time Flies	24
Wintertime Blues	38
Originality	54
Teary Eyed	66
May I Take your Order	76
Criminals of the Night	98
Ancient Ages	108
Disgustingly Sanitary	122
Running Noses	134
Dragons	146
Chocolatey Fudge Pop	158
A Fishy Tale	170
Manhood Choices	182
Little Green Men	196
Theory Index	212

So I Have This Theory...

FOREWORD

Many of the theories represented in this book came to pass during long discussions Caleb and I would have late into the night, mainly during our college days. I would awaken the following day and go to class or study (I am still not sure what Caleb actually did during those college years.) After attending class and reading well-researched scientific theories and laws I would reunite with Caleb and hear his theories pieced together from facts he had gathered from unknown and undocumented sources.

Growing up, I always thought the definition of a fact was uncomplicated. I considered something a fact if it was true and right, or if it had been known to exist or occur. Somehow in our discussions Caleb was able to find "facts" to support any one of his preposterous theories seemingly at any moment.

"Well where did you hear that?" or *"Where did you get that information?"* I would ask. The answer was always, *"that doesn't matter. It is a fact. You can't argue with facts."* *"But what if your fact doesn't make sense?"* I would ask. *"Sorry, it's a fact"* was his response. I would try another approach and attempt to reason scientifically or otherwise about the individual fact presented or attempt to argue the elaborate theory which grew out

of the stated fact. Caleb would respond with, *"Hey, it's a fact. I'm surprised you hadn't heard about this."*

And then the theories, after blossoming, would grow and become more complex and even more difficult to believe, but there was no stopping Caleb. He truly has a unique way of viewing the world. The candor and meticulous intelligence with which he approaches his work is completely squandered by the lunacy of his claims.

It is like someone assembled all the necessary pieces and hardware for a computer but forgot to create a power source. *Imagine watching a television all afternoon without ever turning it on, or imagine traveling many miles and waiting patiently to watch the shuttle launch only to discover that NASA never created an ignition switch.* This is the kind of misdirected intellectual force that you will experience in this book. You may spend hours reading this book and realize that none of it matters, let alone makes any sense. Although you may see the world differently, likely none of your new-found-knowledge will benefit you in anyway or is ultimately true at all.

As a medical doctor, I can't endorse a single theory or thought presented by Caleb in this book.

Caleb's wondering brain and unsound reasoning is evident on every page. I never would have imagined that random facts pondered for hours by a misguided intellect could produce such hilarity.

-Kirk Bodach MD

So I Have This Theory...

INTRODUCTION

Think back to when you were a child and the world was filled with amazing surprises and endless joys of discovery! Clouds formed recognizable shapes as they danced across a flawless blue sky! Large seashells actually stored the sound of the ocean and would play it for anyone who had an ear to listen! Rainbows were astounding treasure maps leading to none other than a gigantic pot of leprechaun gold!

Ah, the blissful days of youth. When crickets actually sang, bedbugs did bite, girls did have cooties, and coffee was still gross! Whatever happened to all of those things that were so magical when we were younger? What happened to the treasure maps, doll houses, and Santa Claus? It all made so much sense when we were younger, the world just fit together so much better.

As we grew older, these ideas and thoughts were slowly drawn out of our minds like poison is drawn from a wound. Labels were given and certainties were established. Words like *"fact," "proof," "never," "always,"* and *"impossible"* began to appear all around us. This type of thinking was new to us and not very agreeable. It forced us to separate ourselves from the wonderful world we thought we lived in, into a world filled only with boring facts and inevitable certainties. Anything outside of these thoughts was merely dismissed as "nonsense." This new world was quite confusing because it maintained signs of the old and interesting world that we used to know.

Ghost stories or Sasquatch sightings reminded us of the world we had loved as children, but strong words like "rumor" or "hoax" quickly forced us to disregard these thoughts or be at risk of being rejected by this new and boring world.

We learned that if we wanted to continue to live among our fellow brothers and sisters of this world, that we must embrace ideas and sayings such as: *"Something is never a fact unless it can be proven; otherwise it is always impossible!"* And the cheers would go up for anyone who would embrace this wonderful new idea that everything did have a logical and sensible answer. Mystery and uncertainty could be defeated! We were finally in control!

So, we went to work, we started with the simple mysteries and continued to work on the trickier ones. We quickly figured out that clouds were not shapes in the sky; they were condensed water vapor forced to move about by high and low pressures in the atmosphere. They were not mystical shapes of cotton floating in the heavens, but vaporous nuisances that brought rain and gloom with them. Awesome... problem solved!

Then, we went to work on ourselves, bent on understanding every single aspect of ourselves and the others around us.

This helped us hush silly rumors like hearing the ocean waves in an old seashell. Now we can proudly stand on any ocean shore and proclaim to the seashell that it has no mystical powers, we are merely hearing an echo of our blood cells flowing past our eardrums. Ha! We rejoice as we toss the seashell into the sand proud that we have lain to rest one more ridiculous rumor.

Rich in knowledge and understanding, we take one glance at a rainbow and laugh at the poor fool who actually believes in leprechauns or pots of gold. We will never fall for such a foolish ruse ever again! We can prove that light shone through water separates the light out into a band of colors that we have named, quantified, and analyzed. We have proof! We have facts! We have truth!

Ah, truth. Truth was never a big issue in the world we used to know, but in this new world of facts, certainties, and absolutes, truth is a must. What is truth however, and what if we prefer not to accept this boring truth over a few exciting unknowns?

The simple answer would be that truth is only what is real and we do not have any choice but to accept it. That argument is not quite strong enough however, so we decided that we must somehow quantify and qualify something as a truth so that it may be analyzed. Naturally, we didn't want to leave room for any loopholes, so we came up with a hypothesis that states: **something is never true unless it can be proven as a fact**; otherwise it remains impossible.

Hooray! The cheers go up once more! Properly defined and categorized truths, now we have a purpose and bright future filled with facts and certainties. But wait, again, we are faced with a dilemma. What if we don't want to cheer for all of these definitions and absolutes?

What if we prefer to think of the world as it used to be, full of wonder, mystery, and Sasquatches. What if we want to believe that there is a pot of gold at the end of a rainbow?

Well my friend, that is precisely what this book is about. I have found quite a few areas in my own life where the simple truth was wholly inadequate. So, instead of giving up and believing boring facts about my existence, I have chosen to spice the truth up a bit. I hope you enjoy it as much as I have. I cannot guarantee that you will learn anything at all, but I do guarantee you a chuckle or two. Enjoy.

-Caleb Zwar

15   So I Have This Theory...

Chapter 1
Migration Patterns

At first glance, one might think this is a complicated theory on the instincts and fascinating habits of migratory waterfowl. Alas, if only I was smart enough to comprehend the complex enigma that surrounds these curious winged beasts of the air, this chapter would definitely be about them. It is not, however. It is about something just as important, if not more so. It is a problem that has driven some men near the point of insanity in their attempt to uncover, or should I say, cover, the answer to this timeless riddle.

What is it that causes perfectly healthy human beings to lose their beloved hair?

"What! Are you kidding me Zwar, baldness, that's the big secret?" Oh sure, belittle it if you must, believe me, I have heard it all before. The world tells us, *"Don't worry about it"* or *"It happens to everyone."* Yet, those of us with receding hairlines, comb-overs, and hair loss treatments cannot help but wonder, *"What is wrong with our heads?"*

I would like to inform you, my lovely reader, that this riddle has taken me years to work out. It was this theory that actually gave me the idea for writing this book. All curses are a blessing in disguise! You just have to know how to look at them.

Well, I would like to start off by putting all of your minds at ease and propose to you not only a soothing and quite comforting theory, which explains not only why we lose our hair, but where it goes when we consider it lost. I am very proud to announce to you my **Hair Migration Theory**.

> **HAIR MIGRATION THEORY:**
> Hair, like all biological entities, grows weary and tiresome over extended periods of time. In its desire for adequate rejuvenation and reprieve, it may choose to relocate itself to less prominent areas for extended periods of rest and solitude.

This theory is not only easy to accept, it warms the heart with the assurance that as you progress in your years and wisdom, you are not merely losing your hair; you are simply allowing it to undergo its natural migratory patterns.

As a child did you ever stop to ponder the shear magnitude of your great-grandfathers eyebrows? Did you ever wonder if when you reached the age of the lovely, old librarian that you may in fact have hair growing out of your ears as well? I need not mention the uneasy feeling found in many young girls as they picture themselves doomed to endure the dreaded chin or mustache hair in their golden years.

Again, let me put all these worries and discrepancies aside as I inform you that your hair, just like every other biological entity, must simply comply with its natural course. The human hair with all of its glands, cells, and nerves cannot possibly be expected to maintain its color, vibrancy, and position forever.

After combing, shampooing, scratching, dying, braiding, and countless other pressures that your hair must undergo every day, week, and year; it needs a break. Not to mention the hats, bandanas, and headphones, that put your hair under a great deal of stress and confusion.

So, what does every living thing desire when undergoing great amounts of stress or difficulties? It seeks out a relief, retreat, or to put it simply, a vacation. Thus, your hair follows the same premise. If we think about this logically we can draw a simple conclusion. I am certain that it is extremely difficult for a single hair to make a valiant stand on the very top of your head, dealing with wind, sun, rain, and all of the other difficulties we discussed earlier. So in simple terms your hair takes a break, a vacation south if you will.

Your hair decides that south is the best direction, much like the Canadian Goose who has determined that the winter is going to be too cold and desolate for its thin little feathers, heads south for the sun and the surf.

Let me inform you, I have not spent tons of money on scientific research to determine how a strand of hair thinks, however, I have a pretty good hunch that it is much easier for a hair to grow out of the ear or nose and deal with a little wax or boogers, than it is to deal with the trials of living the high life on the top of the world.

The nose or eyebrows get just as much attention and oh, how easy it is to be an eyebrow or toe hair. Chin or mustache hair on a female, I admit, a bit unsightly, but what a relief to know that your hair is not gone; it is simply taking a break.

A break, a vacation. Eureka! Is it really that simple? It almost seems too good to be true. Some of us might even regret getting upset and snipping at those renegade hairs trying to escape from our nose or chin. It feels as if we have kicked an old dog off his favorite porch on a sunny day. How many times have we glared in the mirror, frustrated at the thinning of our beautiful head of hair? Frowned at or thought negatively of someone's untended eyebrows or nose-hair? I say rejoice and be glad, you still have all of your hair!

Be sorry for the person whose hair is not on an efficient rotational budget. Mourn for those with full heads of fatigued and weary hair.

Of course, there is nothing perfect in this world; there is a downside to this migration and rotation of hair. Should the fatigued hair become too comfortable in its new environment or setting, it may simply decide to stay in its newly found paradise. We've seen it happen hundreds of times. A person travels south for a vacation and before you know it, that person is looking for condominiums and RV parks surrounded by palm trees.

This reaction can be thwarted however, by encouraging your hair daily to stand firm until refreshed reinforcements can be pulled fresh from the south. No need to trim or cut those relaxing eyebrows or meandering nose-hairs. Let them take their time and before you know it they will be ready to stand firm once again.

No need to thank me dear reader. I know this fantastic theory is life changing to say the least. You may never look at yourself in a mirror the same again. Even if it only puts a smile on your face that's enough for me!

So, throw away those tweezers and trimmers. Let your hair run free like a herd of wild yak on an open prairie. Let your mane roam the open wilderness like a family of gophers in your backyard. Allow your locks to feel free and frolic as they please. Hair-llelujah!!!

So I Have This Theory...

Chapter 2
Time Flies

Flies are curious little creatures, aren't they? They zip around all day and seemingly all night looking for food, trash, or other nasty stuff. Humans and other large critters think of them as annoying and somewhat disgusting pests.

They are always flying, biting, buzzing, tasting, zipping, nipping, and whizzing until *"WHACK!"*
Then, it's twitching, crawling, spinning, limping, and flopping, until finally it's defeated, or is it? Have you ever stopped to see what happens to one of those "wounded" flies after you "get it"?

If you grew up half as curious as I, then I am sure that you have taken the time to simply watch as the twitching fly lays there, then starts wiggling his legs, regains his feet, crawls around for about a minute, and miraculously takes to the air once again! Only to buzz back and forth, over and over again, perhaps even to get whacked yet again.

How can this be?
Do flies have mysterious and mythical healing capabilities?
Are they extremely intelligent and play dead to avoid harm?
Can their bodies withstand incredible amounts of pain and simply endure it?

Not quite my friend, trust me, there is a much more complicated and elusive explanation. However, rest assured that if you pay close attention to my **Time Perspective Theory** it will answer all of these questions as well as others you had no idea existed. By the way, I did say "**Time Perspective Theory.**" Some of you may be thoroughly baffled by this title. I must beg you, do not get lost in the title; there are many other areas in which to get lost.

> **TIME PERSPECTIVE THEORY:**
> The passage of time is not a fixed or definite amount. It varies due to the dimension or perspective in which it is experienced. Speed is relative to the amount of time one has experienced.

Think you've got the idea? Try this one on for size:

"If a dog is four years old, how old is he in human years?"

What does this statement even imply? Years are years aren't they? Is your dog living in an alternate universe or has he found a rift in the space-time continuum? Unless your dog resembles a special breed of Lassie E.T., I believe the answer is undoubtedly no.

Now I know you are already thinking, *"C'mon Zwar, it's because dogs don't live as long as humans!*" You are very correct my auspicious reader. It is because of this difference that we have come to accept that one year in the life of our favorite canine companions is equal to about six or seven years in the life of a human. This makes sense. It helps us understand why old Flash had such a hard time blowing out the candles on his fifteenth birthday bone. It was more like asking a one hundred and five year old man to make a wish and extinguish a forest fire!

"So what's the big deal, some animals live longer than others." You might so eloquently utter. Very true my friend, you are on the right track. Let us consider the other end of the spectrum, sea turtles and land tortoises. Again, curious little creatures, they have an average lifespan of over one hundred and fifty years! Amazing, but how?

Well, let's see if we can't put some things together. Turtles live incredibly long lives, flies live incredibly short lives, dogs are considered old when they are twelve, and some whales are considered middle age when they are seventy.

Can you spot the connection yet? Do you fear this is yet another clueless enigma sent to plague your every pleasant whim, as you lie restless in your bed and slowly become deranged from lack of peaceful slumber? Fear not my knowledge hungry reader… there is quite an obvious link hidden deep within this mystery. Allow me to unveil to you my incredulous findings.

At first, I thought the link must be in the differing species, insect vs. mammal. Put simply, mammals live longer than insects. Mystery solved. Story over. *Wrong!* This theory is riddled with holes. Most troubling, it has no explanation for the differing ages within the species itself.
Example: dog vs. human, both mammals.

Further research sank that theory even deeper with a simple animal called the Hog-Nosed Snipe. When hunted, these little creatures roam over hill and meadow and, as of yet, are only found on Boy Scout outings or church youth trips into the woods. This little creature's life span seems to change daily. Some swear that they live only about 5 years; others claim 50, I've even heard rumors that they only scurry around under a full moon and can live to be over 100 years old!

Out of desperation I turned to the simple facts. What is it that we do know? Let us work from there.

Well, we do know that certain animals live longer than others. Ok, so we know that "time" is one of the variables in this equation, what's next?

Well, how about the animals?

Which ones are living longer, which ones are expiring sooner?

That's when it hit me. It is not the animal's species, type, gender, or color; it's their size!

Size, that's the other variable! Eureka! Now let's see if we can put these two together.

Let's stick with just one species to start with, such as birds. Everyone likes them; they sing us pretty songs and poop on our recently washed vehicles. Let's try out the size proposition on them. Two birds, both hatched from an egg, different sized eggs of course.

Albatross:
Length: 2-4 feet
Wingspan: 7-12 feet
Weight: 50-80 lbs.
Heart Rate: 60-80 beats per minute.
Diet: Squid, Fish, Crabs, Krill, and Algae… (Yummy!)
Average Lifespan: 50-65 years

Hummingbird:
Length: 2-5 inches
Wingspan: 2-3 inches
Weight: 0.1-0.3 ounces
Heart Rate: 250-1250 beats per minute!
Diet: Nectar
Average Lifespan: 2-5 years

I do apologize to the reader. I know that you are reading this book because you want to learn something, and instead I am pummeling you with the true enemy of my book, pure scientific facts. The reason I included this information was not to look like the nerd I used to look like when I was nine, but to draw out the truth behind the "facts." Beware; the real truth behind these facts may not be quite what you are expecting.

Remember that we are looking into the relation between size and time. Well, let's see, the albatross is about 3 feet long, weighs about 70 pounds, and lives about 58 years. Our little friend the humming bird is only about 2 inches long, weighs about 0.2 ounces, and lives about 3 years. This example seems pretty straightforward, the larger an animal is determines how long it will live. However, there must be more to it than that.

Do you suppose that the hummingbird is aware that he is missing out on the extra 55 years that the albatross is getting?

Is the albatross that much happier that he is living almost fifteen times longer than the hummingbird?

Does Fido even have a clue that his owner will probably outlast him a good 50 to 60 years?

Due to the enlightening knowledge found in my **Time Perspective Theory**, I can most certainly tell you that the answer to each of these questions is definitely no.

How can this be?
How can the hummingbird flit happily about the rhododendrons? How can your dog happily wag his little tail? How can a fly even think about enjoying some nicely rotting garbage knowing that in less than a week he will be dead on someone's carpet?

To those of us who expect at least seventy years, these thoughts would be unbearable! But wait, what if we are getting the short end of the stick? Is seventy years long enough? Is life flying by too fast? Peace my good friends. Life is moving just as it should, at it's own pace.

This is an interesting concept; life having it's own pace. I would like to venture forward now in this theory so that you can appreciate the shear and fascinating simplicity hidden in these pages. The answer is in the link between these two premises, *life's natural pace and the pace of natural life.* Am I sounding too much like a boring psychologist? Sorry, let me explain with a few more "facts."

Again, going back to the flies, because everyone loves them. Here are a few things you may not be familiar with regarding the common housefly. The female housefly searches out good, stinky garbage and can lay a couple hundred eggs on it, in about 10 to 18 hours these eggs hatch into cute little baby maggots. Amazingly though, these ugly buggers mature and can fly in less than five days!

They buzz around for 10-15 days if they can avoid the swatter and then its belly up at a ripe old age of 16 days, if they're lucky!

I am not simply telling you this to fill your mind with useless knowledge about houseflies; the point is this. *Have you ever tried to catch a fly with your bare hands?* I have no idea how many hours I have chased a fly around the house only to find him always one step ahead of me. How can such a tiny simple creature out maneuver such a large and witty being such as you and I? The answer is quite simple.

How fast do you think you can move your hand? Even better, how many seconds do you think it takes you to reach out in an attempt to swat at a fly, half of a second, less, maybe? I'll give you the benefit of the doubt and say that you can do it in one quarter of a second. Now that's darn fast.

OR IS IT ONLY FAST TO US?

If it takes 5 days for a fly's egg to turn into an adult, and 12 more days before it is lying belly up on your windowsill, that ¼ of a second may seem much longer to a fly. Actually, if we are sticking with the doggy years factor, ¼ of a second to us is actually the equivalent of about 79,000 seconds in fly time or just short of 22 hours in the bug-eyed kingdom! Makes a bit of a difference doesn't it!

Do you think that if you saw a monstrous human hand descending down at the rate of one inch per hour that you could get out of the way? I have confidence that you would definitely live to fly another day. Think back to my first example, when the cute little fly got "whacked," and after only a few moments was up and flying again? Well, let's apply the theory there shall we.

Think about it, you whack a fly, the fly falls to the ground, twitches around for a few minutes, and then is up and flying again before you know it. Miraculous healing? Nope, just a close case of different time perspectives. To the fly, the "few minutes" he is twitching around is more like 4 to 6 months from his time perspective. We humans can heal just about anything in 6 months, so why can't the fly heal his broken wing or injured feet?

Is my **Time Perspective Theory** beginning to take shape in your knowledge hungry mind? It is not the time that passes. Time is relative to the position and dimension of the viewer. Speed and time are not definite factors. The passage of time feels differently depending on your perspective. If you only have a week and a half to live, like our friend the fly, a couple minutes is all you need to rest, recover, and buzz off again.

Another quick example in which we all can relate is our younger years. Remember when we were younger, and the summer months seemed to last forever. When Christmas and birthdays took ages and ages to arrive. Well, simply apply my **Time Perspective Theory** to this example as well. When you were 7 years old, all you understood about the passage of time were those 7 years. So it really did take 1/7th of your whole life for Christmas or your next birthday to arrive! Later in life, when "time seems to just fly by," it takes a mere 1/55th of your life before Christmas is here again.

Basically, a year doesn't mean what it used to when you only have a couple of years to compare it to.

Is time truly going by faster the older we get? No, simply your perspective of the passage of time has changed. Now that we understand this theory, it is easy to understand why the hummingbird is not disappointed in his short lifespan. To him, his wings beat at a slow and moderate pace and they carry him to a ripe old age. The Bowhead whale, on his 130th birthday, remembers learning to catch krill with his mother as if it were just yesterday.

Do not be sad then for the Housefly whom we feel is doomed to an early death, or for the Tortoise who is forced to watch the years simply drag by. They are both magnificently content. Their little hearts are beating at exactly the pace that God intended, and they go about living life happy just to be alive.

Let us learn from these brilliant creatures and stop worrying about the future, the future will arrive as it always does... right on time.

37   So I Have This Theory...

Chapter 3
Wintertime Blues

I am sure that we have all heard them before:

"Brrr... It's freezing out there!"
"Come out of that weather before you catch your death of cold!"
"Looks like another snow storm is coming."
"Shut that door, you're letting the cold in!"
"I'm freezing my butt off out here!" **and who could forget,**
"I'm so cold, I can't feel my face!"

So what exactly is this list of endless sayings, quotes, and other disgusted utterances? It is simply our verbal way of expressing a common distaste for a very common yet chilling occurrence... cold.

Winter, freezing temperatures, snow, slush, frost, ice... Call it what you may, we all know what it is and despise it. What is it about the cold that makes us all hate it so much? Does it not seem strange that we should all feel such discomfort for something so common and ordinary? I think not, and I am certain that after I have unveiled to you the dark mysteries hidden behind this veil of permafrost, you will quickly warm up to the truth as well.

Oh, I'm sure some of you are now defending, *"C'mon Zwar, winter isn't that bad, snow makes me feel clean and pretty, and Christmas is my favorite."* Give me a break! Christmas is everyone's favorite! Why do you think they stuck it right in the middle of the worst part of the year? Extremely intellectual thinkers believe that we may have Jesus Christ's birth, the real reason for the holiday, off by possibly three years. So what made them plop Christmas in December? A child could answer that one. They knew it would be the only thing that could make the cold winter months bearable.

Let's think about this for a moment. What other options did they have? They knew no one would go outside and light fireworks if Independence Day was in January. Do you think anyone would even care about wearing green if Saint Patty's Day was in December? You don't see anyone carving frozen pumpkins in February do you?

You might be saying to yourself, *"So what,"* or *"That's just the way it is Zwar,"* or even *"I wonder if you can carve a frozen pumpkin?"* Well, I would like to reveal to you not only the importance of properly understanding the implications of this cold conundrum, but also some answers to questions you never dreamed you had.

Mainly, we are going to discuss and understand the severe and adverse effects that cold weather has on individuals, as well as society in general. These effects are minute and subtle, however, I am certain that each of my readers has encountered at least two or three of these effects, and has been at a loss in finding the cause or solution to said effects. However, with a proper understanding of my **Cold Weather Theory**, the mysteries of the ice and drudgery can be fully understood and the full range of their negative effects can be discussed in an intellectual way.

> **Cold Weather Theory:**
> Exposing the human body to prolonged periods of cold temperatures, not only has adverse short-term effects on the body, but can also create long-term, physical and mental damages as well.

First and foremost, I feel the need to define or expound on the definition of cold weather. To some this concept is fairly cut and dry. As for the rest of us, who were not born and raised in Hawaii or Antarctica, we may have a slightly different view on the subject. Let us then begin with the basics.

The human body's normal and healthy temperature is a pleasant 98.6° F. Incredible! That is almost 100° F.

To our human bodies, this is normal or average temperature. Anything less is perceived by our senses as subnormal or below average. Therefore, we can safely state that as a human species any temperature less than 98.6° F is perceived as cold. If this isn't sinking in yet, let's look at it a different way.

Our bodies are composed of almost 70% water content. 70% water! Again, amazing! Water is made up of two hydrogen atoms and one fatty oxygen atom. Water is an interesting compound because it never stops moving. In its liquid state it is constantly bouncing around and shouting, *"hollers"* to its other molecular homeboys. Now here's the kicker. Water does slow down as it approaches its freezing point, which just so happens to be 32° F. At this point the happy little water molecules slow down so much that they actually freeze in place. A substance we normally call ice.

Here's the short and skinny. We humans are 70% of a substance that freezes solid at 32° F.

Now I don't know if you have ever taken a look at the thermometer during one of those "pretty little snowfalls," but I can bet you seven cents that it was below the freezing point of water. So what do we do? We put on a cute little hat and some knitted mittens, and go frolicking through this "winter wonderland". Wonderland indeed!

Let us look at what happens on our return from this frigid venture. We come tumbling in from the outside, covered in extra layers of "insulation," crying about frozen noses, chattering teeth, or even frostbitten toes. We shiver, shake, and complain about how cold it is and how we can't feel certain appendages. We never apologize to our shaking or frozen extremities for exposing them to sub-frigid temperatures.

Do you think it's possible that for the last few thousand years our bodies have been giving us clues as to the negative effects of cold on our bodies? Could it be that all of their shivering, shaking, and chattering responses to our ignorance have been in vain? I am certain that if our bodies could speak they would resound in an exuberant "YES!"

Never fear however, the purpose of this book is to allow you the reader to discover more about yourself and the world around you. Thus, my **Cold Weather Theory** is the perfect thing to cure your wintertime blues. Like most of my theories I will prove my point to you, not through scientific facts or expensive, experimental trickery, but with numerous amounts of exuberant and intellectual utterances. This will allow you to presume my credentials on the subject in hopes of proving to you the validity of my desired proposition. Now that we have that settled, let us begin with a scenario with which I am sure many of you are familiar.

Imagine yourself walking through the park, freshly fallen snow slowly settling over the trees and the sidewalk. You see a happy little squirrel dancing merrily through the billowy, white carpet leaving only small tracks as it scurries up a nearby oak tree. You glance at his steep ascent and take notice of the slow, rhythmic song as the tree limbs dance in the winter breeze. The only sound for miles is the muffled crunch of your footsteps in the freshly fallen snow. You marvel at the beauty of your surroundings, so quiet and frozen in place. A light rushing sound announces a gust of wind as it chases itself through the powder covered trees and shrubs. You tighten your jacket as you pull your chin to your chest and warm your hands with a long breath of damp warm air. As you rub your hands together and plunge them into your pockets a thought crosses your mind. **"It sure is cold out here!"**

Amazing! *"It sure is cold out here!"* No joke, look who's talking. As you tramp through your little "snow playground" staring at squirrels and shrubs, what do you think 70% of your hydrated body is doing? Do you think that it is just looking around at all of the happy little frozen water molecules and saying: *"Hey guys look its snowing, how gorgeous!"* or *"Let's go sledding!"* or how about *"This cold air is so refreshing!"* Nice try! I am very sad to say that this is not even close. In fact, I am convinced that their little molecular conversation resembles something more like this:

H_2: *"Look Billy, frozen bodies everywhere!"*
O: *"Don't talk now Judy, just try to keep moving, just keep moving!"*
H_2: *"I can't feel my atoms Billy!"*
O: *"Don't give up on me now!"*
H_2: *"Find a warm place… Find a warm place…"*
O: *"Please, for the love of ionic bonds, get us out of here!"*
H_2: *"I'm fading fast Billy"*
O: *"Quick hold my electron Judy"*
H_2: *"I'll never forget you Bi…"*
O: *"JUDY! Noooooo…"*

The rest is just too disturbing for me to put into words. Trust me; it is not a happy ending! If this startling representation alarms you, as it should, you are beginning to understand the true horror behind this icy charade.

So, we now realize that our bodies are under attack by the cold at the molecular level, but how about on a larger scale? Well, let's see.

Again picture yourself walking along the street, possibly heading back to the office after lunch. There is snow flying in all directions as you step into a nearby pool of slush. The wind picks up rapidly, tearing through your coat and hat. You instinctively scrunch up your shoulders and pull your collar around your neck and chin as you trudge on.

You finally reach the office door, shoes soaked, fingers numb, ears and nose bright red, and all this accompanied by a sore neck and back.

Does this scenario sound familiar, perhaps too familiar? I would venture to say that if you have ever lived in an area of the world that receives snowfall, even once a year; you would know exactly how this person feels after trudging through the cold. Exhausted, stressed out, and irritable. Why? How could a simple jaunt through the cold bring about such ill feelings and negative emotions? Since your simple mind is at a loss, allow me to explain.

Let us begin by discussing the three main areas that are commonly affected by the cold. First, the hands. Possibly one of God's most amazing creations. They allow us to tie ties, flick flies, and cover our eyes.

Without them we could never draw doodles, pet poodles, or eat noodles. That's not to mention tickling toes, picking our nose, and slapping hands with bros (in that order).

Hands are simply incredible. They are made up of thousands of delicate nerves and tissues that allow us to create some of the world's greatest works of art. And yet, we take them outside, put little cloth coverings over them, and expect these amazingly complex creations to be simply peachy. I am sorry to say that we have been sorely mistaken. Our wonderful little fingers go numb because the life giving blood cells refuse to flow through them. Then we force them to make balls of snow and hurl them through the air, only to get upset when our aim is off. *Off indeed!*

The next vital area is our legs and feet. These poor little troopers never say die, and yet we relentlessly drive them through the slush and snow. Think of it, their job is to carry not only their own weight, but also the weight of the entire body. For some, this is an easier job than for others. As if that were not enough, we then decide to simply cover our legs with a little khaki or denim material and proclaim that we are ready to go. The feet have it even worse; they are covered with a thin stocking, shoved into a smelly thin leather shoe, and plunged repeatedly through the snow and slush. This causes our poor unfortunate little toes to be refused the circulation and warmth they need as they pass slowly into their own little metatarsal comas.

Lastly, and quite possibly the most important, are the misfortunes of our back, neck, and shoulders. Think about it.

As we make our way along through the sadness of winter, we tend to shuffle along looking at the ground as we tighten our shoulders and neck in a desperate attempt to trap any escaping heat.

This process is ultimately futile and usually results in our body violently convulsing in allergic reactions to the cold itself. We so timidly refer to this process as "shivering." What a shameful misconception! This allergic reaction combined with tightened back and neck muscles causes stress and pain that continues on even after we are warmed in our nice cozy houses. These complications escalate into headaches, back-pains, and ill-tempered behavior.

What can we do then to change our misconceptions of the frozen evil that plagues us?
Is it even possible to escape something as vast and imposing as cold?
Have we humans always been subdued by this seemingly ever-present dilemma?

I realize the somewhat upsetting situation we are faced with. However, I would like to assure you that there is no need to panic. This so-called "thorn in our flesh" can be removed, and if proper precautions are taken, we need not fear its icy grip ever again.

Let us take a look back in time. Say around the year 1492. Many of us are familiar with this date and its meaning. I like to brag that 65% of my readers are fairly intellectual beings and would know this as the date in which Columbus made his famous discovery of the Americas. Or did he really? Actually, he didn't land on the mainland of North or South America, but on an island in the Caribbean. Why didn't he land in Maine or perhaps Canada, the trip would have been shorter? Could it be they did not want to discover another cold land? "Isolated incident", you might say.

Aright, let us go farther back. Say around 2200 BC. A Biblical story, which takes place in an area, called "the Fertile Crescent." This is an area near what used to be the Tigris and Euphrates River deltas, an area with rich soil and splendid wildlife; a place one might call a natural paradise. What we find is a large group of humans who are unwilling to leave this perfect area and go explore the ends of the earth. So, they get together and build themselves a tower to stay ahead of the Jones'. What happens? God Himself must change their languages and break their little toy tower just so they will leave their paradise and eventually venture out into the cold. They had no plans of doing it on their own. Don't believe me? You can read about it in Genesis 11.

So what are we to assume? God wanted us to live in the frozen tundra? Not at all my friends, think of where he put us when he made us. For those of us who were not listening during Sunday school, the answer is the famous "Garden of Eden".

On the sixth day God created man and placed him in an igloo? Nope. In a snowstorm? Not hardly. The truth is, he put us in a garden filled with warm plants and trees, probably palm trees, surrounded by wonderful fruits and streams. He also did not supply Adam and Eve with much of a wardrobe either, a perfect hint to the naturally warm temperature. This gives us a good idea of what God thinks is a great climate for humans to thrive in as well.

Can you hear the collective sigh of so many hands, feet, necks, backs, noses, ears, fingers, and toes? Finally, a voice for the mute, crying out in desperation for anyone who will listen and make a decision to care for these neglected wounds. Wounds that begin on the surface, yet overtime seep down to steal the very spring in our step. May we no longer stand by, in the cold and allow our bodies to shiver themselves into a state of sadness and solitude.

I want you to put down this book right now and give yourself a big hug. Apologize for all of the pain and sadness you have put it through over the years. Go ahead do it, I'm not kidding! Next, explain to your body your prior ignorance on the subject and rejoice in your new revelation.

Depending on the amount of hurt or damage you have inflicted over the years, it may take some time before your body is ready to forgive your actions and move on. A great place to start is by establishing neutral ground that you and your body can agree on.

Some suggestions your body may offer could sound a little something like this, *"Hey you, let's move to Florida!"* or *"I've heard that Fiji is nice this time of year"* or even *"Surfs up you coat wearing bozo!"* Probably the most important tip of all is to start today. Don't deprive your body of warmth for one more day.

If all of these steps are followed correctly, I cannot guarantee you a happier life, but I can ensure that you will have peace of mind, knowing that your body is happy and temperate. I believe that you will also begin to see the long term effects of cold upon your body simply vanish into warm air. Possible back and neck pain may decrease, which may result in fewer headaches and stress.

So act today, stop ignoring your body and its incessant pleas for warmth and freedom. Put your foot down and get the temperature up!

53   So I Have This Theory...

Chapter 4
Originality

Originality. It is the creation or conception of any brand spanking new thought or idea in which no previous person has ever conceived or contrived previously. Spectacular isn't it! Everyone loves a new idea, an ingenious new invention, or of course, a fantastic new discovery. New stuff is exciting! Who isn't exhilarated by the innovation of a new concept or theory? You and I both know that the Zwar himself absolutely adores a new, cutting-edge theory!

How amazing it is to live in an era where we see so many new developments and new inventions everyday! What a splendid time to be alive!

Why, just the other day I was on my way to see the new movie *"Oceans Thirteen,"* when I saw the brand new Dodge Charger drive past. My buddy commented that he liked the new Charger almost as much as the new redesigned Ford Mustang. As we continued on, we saw a billboard advertising the new fall fashion; the all-new vintage tweed jacket, and never before seen bell-bottom faded pants. Not caring too much about our fashion we continued on to the theatre. Upon arriving, we found that our movie was sold out, but that didn't bother us we had plenty of brand spanking new movies to check out.

They were showing:
- *"Saw 7"*
- *"Dukes of Hazard 2"*
- *"Starsky & Hutch 2"*
- *"Lion King 2 ½"*
- *"Star Wars Episode 3"*
- *"Spider Man 3"*
- *"Batman Begins Again"*
- *"X-men 3"*
- *"The Return of King Kong the Sequel 2."*

Unbelievable! How would we find the time to watch all these great, brand new movies?

As we stood there clueless as to which new movie we should go see, my buddy muttered, *"Where do they get all their great ideas for all these new movies?"* Due to the fact that I was craving a large Mountain Dew and a king size bag of Sour Patch Kids, I simply muttered back a simple, *"I don't know man?"* This question began to haunt me however as we sat and watched, *"The Return of Freddy vs. Jason 6."*

What I could not forget, if you haven't figured it out already, is that all of the new ideas, inventions, and creations surrounding us in today's media, news, and readers digest are no more than cleverly disguised remakes.

Reproductions.
Recreations.
Rip Offs.

Oh, of course the "artists" of today do not call them that. They have established much more pleasant terms for their clever rip-offs. They use words like, "redesigned," "improved," "retro," "vintage," "re-mastered," and my favorite "new!" Sometimes if they are really in a pinch, they might even combine a few of them.

"Come drive the New Redesigned SUV today!"
"Try our New and Improved odor resistant insoles!"
"Now, see all your favorite movies Re-mastered and Improved!"
"The New Retro look is in!"

What is the matter with you people? Do you know what "new" means? Well, here's a hint, it doesn't mean that it existed before or that it can be re-anythinged! Now, before I get all riled up, I must tell you that I did not uncover this on my own; sadly, I was drawn in just like the millions of other earthlings watching remakes and buying new and improved stuff everyday. What jolted me into the sad reality was none other than a comment from a friend at a movie!

Believe it or not, we were going to watch "The Fast and Furious 2," (obviously before "The Fast and Furious 3 and 4" came out) when I commented on the abnormal amount of remakes found in the media today. My friend didn't seem phased by my question whatsoever, he simply shrugged and stated,

"Yeah, that because in the year 1999, the world officially ran out of ideas."

Of course at the time we all chuckled; at this comment, the world running out of ideas, what foolishness. Even so, I could not seem to forget this comment. Instead, I decided to nail down the cause for this blatant reproduction of ideas. It took me almost five years to reach a proper understanding of this ridiculous phenomenon, and these are my findings:

> **Originality Theory:**
> We as a human race have grown lazy in the creation and discovery of new ideas and thoughts. We have grown accustom to re-making old ideas and are in danger of losing our creative and artistic abilities all together.

"Oh my, is this possible?" you might be muttering to yourself. Luckily for you, with a proper understanding of my **Originality Theory**, you can understand the trap that lurks behind every new idea, and break free of the downward spiral of re-creations in which we are caught today. My hope is that with this knowledge we can make this planet a much better place to create in. If anything else, hopefully we will come up with a new idea or two.

Now, I know what you are thinking right now, *"The Zwar is just getting carried away. We have new stuff come out all the time!"* Allow me to clear up this common misconception for all the weak and timid minded creatures out there. We live in a time where words carry shockingly little value. So what have we done to overcome this issue? We have simply compounded our usage of terminology in order to stress their importance in numbers. For example, if a company comes out with an altered design of a pre-existing toothbrush, they no longer can simply promote it by saying:

"Try the redesigned toothbrush; it still cleans just like the old one!"

No, no, no! Who would want to buy this? So, what do they do when their words don't quite pack the same punch as the original? They simply throw in a few adjectives to spice things up:

"Try the new and improved toothbrush; you too could feel the difference today!"

Well, it's a little better; at least it is "new" and "improved." I am not sure how you can have something that is both new and yet improved, but that's another story. The problem still remains that it doesn't quite jump out at the general audience. So, they go ahead and give it a cool new name and capitalize a few words here and there:

"You too Must try the New and Improved Oral B9 PlaqueBuster Today! Find out what you could be missing!"

Oh my, that does sound impressive! The Oral B9 PlaqueBuster, Wow!

My current toothbrush doesn't blast any plaque, so maybe they've got something. It's still no good however. There's too many maybe's, and not enough proof or certainty. People want to know that they are going to see results. No problem! They want results? We can make some up:

"Buy the New and Improved Oral B9 PlaqueBuster Today and See the Difference Tomorrow! Feel Better, Smile Brighter, and Improve your Life Today! You owe it to your Teeth!"

And all of a sudden you find yourself thinking,

"Wow, I must buy an Oral B9 PlaqueBuster! I don't care how much they cost. I honestly don't know how I have made it this long without one? I have been feeling a bit down lately, it must be that old ratty toothbrush that has been ruining my life! Thank-you Oral B9 PlaqueBuster, Thank-you!!"

Now, what just happened here? There was nothing wrong with our toothbrush at the beginning of this ridiculous ad campaign, and now, all of a sudden, we are convinced that our old, dilapidated toothbrush is the cause of all of our life's grief and misfortune. How did we arrive at this point? Simple, we were merely verbally bombarded to death until our prior understanding gave way to the smokescreen of adjectives, italics, titles, and blatant verbologies! Lies are what we used to call them. Now they are referred to as opinions, embellishments, or marketing schemes.

Why all the embellishments? Why do we need all the marketing schemes? The answer is quite simple; we don't have any new ideas. Correct me if I am wrong but isn't the, "Fantastically New and Improved Oral B9 PlaqueBuster," still only a simple toothbrush? Oh, I admit, it may have a cool color or squiggly mark here and there, but it's still just a toothbrush. Not much different from the toothbrush that my Grandfather used back when he was my age. Interesting.

So, instead of inventing a new toothbrush, or inventing anything for that matter, we focus all of our time and creative energy into complicated marketing and promotional schemes. We flood billboards, commercials, and magazines with the same products we already have, only now they are sporting new names, colors, or squiggle marks. Some of these products were actually invented years and years ago and have simply been re-marketed ever since.

To me, this is highly upsetting! You may not think so now, but just think a few years down the road. Sure, maybe for now we can keep "re-designing" and "re-making" old ideas and old inventions. But what happens when we run-out of things to "re-make" or "re-design?"

We have already "re-made" five "King Kong" movies. We've already "re-introduced" the last 50 years of clothing fashions and we still drive machines that were invented over 100 years ago.

Oh sure, 6.2 billion people in the world and one guy comes up with something new called an iPod, and we think that next year we are going to be flying to Mars or teleporting to each others houses. Wake up people! I understand that "re-designing" or "re-making" something takes little to no money and even less brain power, but it leaves us spiraling downward toward a lazy existence filled with empty promises and piles of old recycled and re-introduced junk!

"Don't re-Invent the Wheel," has become synonymous with, **"Don't spit into the wind,"** and **"Don't whizz on the Electric Fence!"**

If we truly are sincere in our pursuit of producing a truly new and unique product that we can proudly pass on from generations to come, we must "re-invent" the wheel entirely!

Do you think that Edison took a little stroll through the "Lighting Fixtures" section of Home Depot before he rolled up his sleeves and got to work? Or did Ford simply look at the 1850's model and decide which features to keep and which to scrap on the "Newly Redesigned Model T?" I'm sure that Beethoven and the Beetles would have done just fine if they went with remixes and remakes instead of their original tunes.

If you haven't gotten the point by now, I fear you never will my friend. In short, original thinking is what makes us human. Aping is the act of copying others out of shear stupidity! I cannot make this decision for you. Each true artist must choose to labor through the pain, failure, and triumph of creating something entirely unique and profoundly original, or else we are all doomed to a bland future filled with counterfeit ideas and someone else's dreams!

I can only assure you that the joy resulting in triumphing over something that you have labored over for ages has no greater reward than simply knowing that you can do something yourself.

So get out there and "re-invent" as many wheels as you can find! Be original, by being original!

So I Have This Theory...

Chapter 5
Teary Eyed

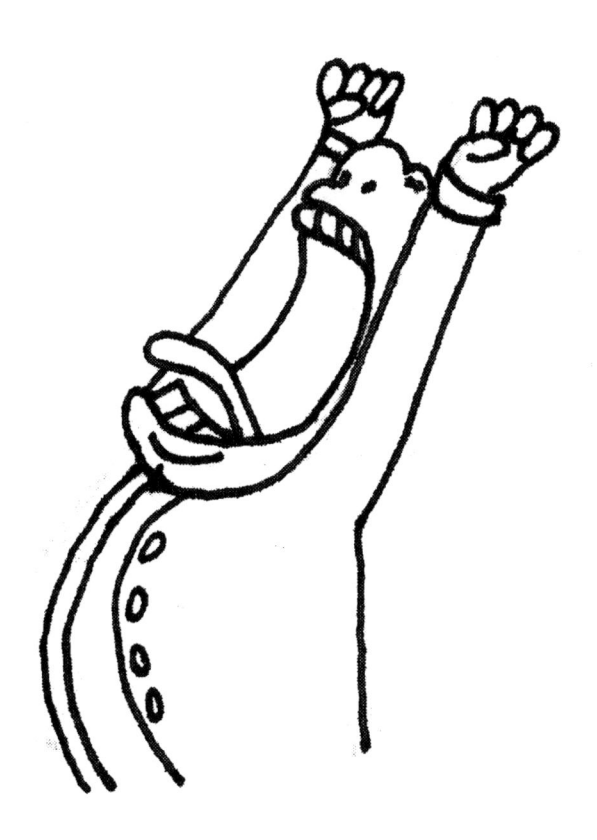

A yawn. What an interesting phenomenon. When combined with a good stretch, we feel we are completely relaxed and ready to doze right off. When exercised at inappropriate times however, yawns can get us into deep trouble. A yawn during an interview, or client meeting is considered quite rude and out of place. Who can forget the implications of a misplaced yawn while enduring a long epilogue from a significant other about the travesty that occurred earlier in his or her day?

In short, yawns portray messages like, *"I am tired," "I don't care,"* **or** *"I am not interested."*

I find this quite unsettling! Especially when the general public has no explanation or true understanding as to the origin or purpose of a yawn. A recent survey of three individuals shows the void of knowledge surrounding this subject, as well as the discrepancy between varying views. Two out of the three individuals had no explanation whatsoever to the origin or reaction which take place before, during, and after a yawn. The third merely smiled and continued to walk away, obviously baffled and shocked into silence at the possible cosmic implications of this enigma.

This mystery, which has lasted through countless years of space and time, innumerable misunderstandings, and who knows how many "excuse me" indications, can now be unveiled and appreciated for its simplicity and entirety. Never again will the simple yawn be misunderstood or considered untimely and rude. Here is my explanation:

> **Yawn Theory:**
> **The triggering mechanism that results in the familiar stretching of the oral cavity known as yawning, originates in the ocular cavity. This common stretching exercise has multiple side effects, the most important of which, is the lubrication of the visual sensory devices.**

This proposition does take some thought to understand and appreciate its intricacies. I also feel the need to discuss other popular ideas and theories on the subject. Such as, *"Your lungs need more air when you get tired to keep you awake,"* or the ever ridiculous, *"Your brain needs more oxygen."* I need not say much about these ideas due to the fact that my readers are not easily duped into believing such malarkey or shenanigans based only on scientific tests and analysis. I simply felt the need to address these ideas to show how some may use smoke and mirror tricks to create solutions for problems that baffle even the greatest of minds.

So, let us dive in shall we! The first element in understanding my

Yawn Theory is to determine when yawns occur. Any simpleton can easily deduce that yawns occur when the individual is tired, fatigued, or sleepy. Yawns are seldom found frolicking in the park, dancing in the rain, or cutting a rug on the dance floor.

Let's continue this adventure of the mind. What happens to us when we are tired? Let's see, our memory suffers, we zone out from time to time, we get the munchies, our eyes get dry and droopy… that's it!! Our eyes! Every person must admit that every time they get sleepy or tired their eyes become dry, irritable, and refuse to remain open.

Now you might be wondering, *"Alright Zwar, I thought we were talking about yawning. What's that got to do with the eyes?"* Everything! Unlike the common, accepted belief of yawns related to the lack of oxygen in the brain, (quite balderdash I can assure you) the truth is that yawns are actually triggered by our eyes! Now listen, before you get all riled up. I realize the truth is hard to accept at times, however, do not let minor things such as scientific and medical proof cloud your mind from the actual facts hidden beneath.

"I don't believe it!" you mutter. What's that? Unbelief, oh I hope so! I hold my readers to a much higher standard than to simply accept any

whim or wisp of truth that floats down the stream of life. You are highly intellectual beings and a highly intellectual explanation in required. Feeling better? May I continue? Thank you.

We've touched on the fact that when you are tired your eyes desire moisture and your eyelids just aren't cutting it! So let's now look at how the yawn helps to accomplish this moisturizing task. It is a fairly complicated process so I will not obscure the topic by using frivolous explanations. To sum up, the yawn creates pressure to equalize the nasal area. This causes the tear ducts to overflow. The result, happy and moisturized eyes! The trigger to the yawn is the key that unlocks this strange mystery.

How many times has it happened to you?

You and your friend are carrying on a perfectly normal conversation about the anti-gravitational properties of terrestrial beings in a two-dimensional environment, and mid-sentence your friend covers his mouth concealing a perfectly normal yawn and follows it up with a pleasant, "excuse me." Next thing you know your mouth is gaping open, tongue is hanging out, eyes are squinting, and you are gasping for air while you utter something like, "You got me," or "Stop yawning."

Let me ask you another question. How did you know that your friend was yawning? Hmmm? *"What do you mean? We were just talking,*

I probably saw him yawn, I don't know?" You nailed it my friend, you probably saw him. One last question, if you saw him yawn, do you think your eyes saw the yawn as well? I truly hope that you get this one right. The answer of course is yes! Most definitely!

So if you are already tired and fatigued and your eyes are getting dryer by the minute, do you honestly think they won't jump at the chance of obtaining even a drop of moisture giving tears? Should they merely look on in agony as they witness another's eyes bathe in the sweet delight of moisture?

Apparently you do! You not only excuse your eyes for their ridiculous behavior in obtaining minor refreshment, you scold the other person and order them to stop allowing their eyes minor pleasures as well.

It's like riding a camel across the desert for three days and then placing it in front of a fresh bubbling spring, only to scold it and push its head away every time it goes for a drink.

Despair no longer however, there is hope. My **Yawning Theory** is not meant to leave your eyes merely wallowing in their dryness and sorrow. A proper understanding always leads to correct choices. *"And knowing is half the battle!"* (As my 80's upbringing will attest.) So now that we understand our folly, we can now make steps in the right direction. There are really only two major steps to this healing process; courtesy and pride.

The first and most overlooked is yawn courtesy. Think of a sneeze, when you have a good sneeze what do you do? Think about it, what usually follows up your first sneeze? Exactly! A second sneeze or even a third. Many times when the second or third sneezes do not occur, we will stop and prepare for them just in case they may decide to go for it. This is proper sneeze etiquette.

Yawning should follow the same rule. If you have one good open-mouthed, drooling yawn, don't cup your hand over it or dismiss it with a quick shake of your head. Embrace it and pause in case another is on the way.

The second step in the healing process, pride. I turn again to sneezes.

When someone accomplishes a good clean snot flinging sneeze what is the first thing out of our mouth?

"God Bless You!"
"Gesundheit!"
"Mazel Tov!"

We praise the sneeze! We bless the sender and utter other words of which we don't even know the meaning! This makes the sneeze feel welcome and if we are lucky this praise may even trigger a second more boisterous sneeze. On the other hand, we do just the opposite with yawns. We hide them, excuse them, and just plain make them feel terrible for coming. We must praise them as well. We must thank them for their help and marvel at their beauty!

Let us put an end to eye drops and rewetting solution. Let us allow our body to accomplish its tasks without ridicule and shame. We must bless the yawn as well, and be proud of its effects. May there be no more dry or red eyes in the world.

Let your jaw hang wide and your praise ring loud. Freedom for the tears of the world!

Teary Eyed 74

So I Have This Theory...

Chapter 6
May I Take Your Order?

"May I take your order?" How many times have you been asked this very question? Now before you start counting and get off track let me just tell you, I don't really want to know. What I would like to know, however, is why does this simple question bring us so much irritation and grief? Not sure what I am babbling on about? Alright then, simply think back to the last time you were asked this same question.

Waiter: *"May I take your order?"*
You: *"Well now, I think we might just need another minute or two."*

Waiter: *"May I take your order?"*
You: *"Yeah, I uh… well… I'll have the… uh… oh, what is your soup of the day?"*

Waiter: *"May I take your order?"*
You: *"Um, yes, I'll start with water… and, what are your specials again?"*

See what I mean, drama. What is this incredible dilemma that faces us every time someone simply tries to take our order? Could it be the uncertainty of decision? Perhaps it is the fear of choosing something unlovely?

Whatever it is we are deathly afraid of surrendering our order to anyone. Whoa, wait a tick... surrendering our order eh? Interesting... I think we may have found something. Perhaps it is not the decision or the choice that makes us falter.

Maybe it is something much deeper and vastly more mutinous. Perhaps we should be examining each part of the question and its deeper implications.

"May I take your order," seems simple enough to start with... or is it? Let's break it down shall we. Perhaps, we can find what lies hidden beneath this coded conundrum of terror.

"May"= verbal auxiliary / have permission or liberty to

"I"= pronoun / the one speaking or writing

"Take"= verb / to get into one's hands or possession: GRASP, SEIZE

"Your"= adjective / of or relating to you or yourself

"Order"= noun / the prevailing state of things: ARRANGEMENT, REGULARITY

So, if we decipher the true coded message we find something like this: *"Can I have the liberty to seize or grasp my hands on your state of arrangement or regularity?"* Wow! Not quite what it sounded like in the Burger Castle drive-thru is it? See, our highly advanced minds are not duped into believing this clever twist of phraseology. We have never been comfortable with this little question and now we can clearly understand why. Another question arises however, why is our order so darn important to us? Well my good friends, the facts are as plain as the nose on a donkey!

> **Human Order Theory:**
> We as humans have cultivated and established a list of rules and guidelines by which we hold ourselves in restraint, and have come to fear what is outside of these boundaries. Only through breaking these regulations can we begin to expose and overcome them.

Ok, I realize that there are a bunch of big words there so let's start by making this as simple as possible. We humans have established, over many years, a certain creed or set of guidelines that we expect others to simply follow. We usually enforce these policies stating things like, *"that's just the proper way to do things"*. These rules disguise themselves in various ways but all lead back to the same underlying theme. What is this theme my friends? Hold on to your kneecaps!

We humans are addicted to order! It's true! No dancing around this fact my friends, the signs are everywhere. We are hopelessly enthralled with the idea of order, perfection, uniformity, flawlessness, regularity, or to sum them all up, blatant normality!

If there is any doubt in your minds, you have simply to look around you and see the thousands of attempts we humans have made at trying to make this imperfect world, in which we live, perfect and flawless. We do it everywhere! If you still cannot bring yourself to admit the truth let me ask you a few loaded questions:

Why do we mow our lawns and then spread fertilizer over them?
Why do we get out of our beds and insist on making them again?
Why can't you wear a brown belt with black shoes?
Why do we use soap to clean a painted, metal car?
Why do we hide the toilet brush and plunger from visitors?
Why can't I wear sneakers to work?

**Why must we chew with our mouth closed?
Why do we have scented toilet paper?
Why can't you stare at strangers?
Why do we put soap in a dish, will it get dirty?**

So, what exactly is going on here? Has the entire human race gone loopy? Quite possibly! Now, I am certain that a few of my more critical readers may have an answer for perhaps one or two of the ridiculous nuances listed above. However, if we were forced to give a detailed explanation for each one of these strange behaviors, I am almost certain that each one of us would indeed, fall quite short. Still, we all follow similar guidelines to these every single day. Why follow a set of rules you can't explain?

Well, never fear my befuddled readers, I have discovered quite an astounding answer to all of these questions and perhaps many more! This discovery not only uncovers shocking truths about the world around us, it also unveils the hidden truth behind the many oddities we find in ourselves. What oddities you ask? Read on, and be utterly amazed!

Even at a young age the idea of order is branded into us much like cattle branding on an old ranch. This type of branding is very subtle and may be administered without either party ever being aware of its influence. Of course, similar to a plague, it begins very small. Per-

haps just a word here and there:

"Alice, try and color inside the lines next time."

"Let's all gather around kids and sit in a nice, neat circle."

"Make sure to sit up straight like a good girl."

"Johnny, pick up your toys, we are expecting company."

"Quiet down children and form a straight line."

"Tommy, let's put the lid on the glue and stop eating it."

"Go clean your room like a good girl."

"Billy stop picking your nose and flicking bogies at your sister!"

Now I just wonder, can a highly impressionable child hear comments like these day after day and not begin to believe that he or she will be doomed if they step outside of this invisible circle of neatness? What might happen if he or she dared to deviate from this narrow course of perfection? Perhaps the child thinks, *"If I just try hard enough and follow all these rules, I can grow up and be perfect like all the big people!"*

Oh sad day! At what age do you think little Bobby and Susie will find out that all the sitting up, line forming, circle sitting, toy cleaning, shushing, and non-nose picking in the world will lead you to the exact same end as all the other little kids who did not refrain from such crude indulgences?

What prize will they have to show for their cheerless childhood free of dirt, noise, adventure, laughter, and boogers?

Will they ever become those "perfect big people" who instructed them every inch of the way?

Will they reach that great land of rewards that awaits all the good little behaved boys and girls?

I believe you and I both know the saddening answer to this sick and twisted riddle. I believe we call it "childish" behavior for a reason don't you?

Now, I know what you may be thinking, *"But I'm not one of those old cranky people who yell at kids to be proper and behave."* Good for you!

How would you describe yourself then? *"Well, I'm a nice person, I help out whenever I can, and I like to have my share of fun too."*

Come on man! Don't you see, "nice person", "share of fun", "help if I can", these are all perfect examples of the early "order brandings" you received from childhood. What happened to the "dangerously exciting", "crazy fun", and "I'll be there, no matter what" kind of attitude? Where did the "stay up all night", "try anything once", and "go for broke" mentality go? If you think I am using harsh language right now, then you are in more of a critical condition then you may even be aware!

What keeps a person hooked on this life of order and perfection once they see that it is completely unattainable? The answers are all around you my friends. Others!

You and I are the keepers of this heinous, repetitive crime. We are simply afraid. Afraid of stepping out of line for fear of what others may think of our incredible insurrection. Afraid of what lies beyond the great circle of cleanliness and perfection.

So what do we do? We continue along the endless path of desiring to be wild and crazy, yet also desiring to be thought of as normal and ordinary. Day and night we have order, normality, and organization pounded into our heads. We are completely surrounded and submersed in a world addicted to order.

Don't believe me? Think I'm exaggerating? Read on if you dare, but I must warn you what I am about to unveil to you might be disturbing to a few of my more clean and tidy readers. If at this point you need to take a break for a tall glass of water, I would most definitely recommend you do so.

Now that you are hydrated, let's continue with an area in which I'm sure most of us are familiar, the business world. I am certain I do not even need to illustrate what would happen to the business or professional world if order or regularity were compromised even for one single day.

You have not seen a truly sad individual until you have seen a businessman who is late for work with spilled coffee on his shirt only to arrive and find he has forgotten his cell phone and can't get his PDA to turn on. What a cruel world we live in.

How about all of the things we humans have created to "help" maintain our precious order in our businesses or professions. Let's see, we first make sure that all of our sidewalks and roads are in as many straight lines as possible. What a horror it would be if we had to go out of our way to get to the mailbox!

We have even labeled our favorite computer activity as, "going on-line". How many different names or threats have we tossed at our poor, defenseless computers if they dare to kick us "offline", or take more than twenty seconds to connect us to the rest of the world?

Let's switch gears for a minute and simply marvel at a few of the terms and sayings with which we are all very familiar. I am sure that each of us has used these terms without even thinking of the long term affects they might have on all those around us. These are but a taste of what is truly out there, but they should give you somewhat of an idea of the filth we utter on a day-to-day basis!

"Don't step out of line!"
"He's a real straight shooter!"
"Take some time to get things in order!"
"Watch him, he's a crooked individual!"
"Just give me a straight answer!"
"Let's keep a nice regular pace!"
"Straighten up and fly right!"
"I like him, he's as straight as an arrow!"
"Keep your eyes forward!"
"Sit up straight!"
"Follow the straight and narrow!"
"It's going to be smooth sailing from here!"
"Having trouble staying regular…?"

This list just goes on and on! We have not only created words and phrases that are as common as cereal commercials, but they are also just as catchy. We have begun to start believing that this ridiculous perfection is actually attainable and waiting for us, just around the bend. The funny thing is, if we ever reached that point, would we even have the courage to abandon our straight and narrow path and venture around the bend anyway?

My last point on this little nugget of knowledge is to describe to you irrevocable proof of our utter addiction to order in none other than a game. Quite a few games in fact. Games so important that we no longer call them games but sports!

Sports are quite interesting little activities. Some are a great matching of skill and talent, others a show of physical strength and a great source of exercise. But I would like to focus on the creation and purpose of the sports, rather than the athletes who participate in them.

Confused? Good! What I am trying to get at is this. As we have grown older and wiser, we have found that no amount of clean living, good planning, or nose blowing is going to lead us to a life of perfection where nothing bad or unexpected happens. So what do we do?

Give up; throw in the towel on perfection? Not a chance, we are humans, we always have the answer! We simply decided to create a world in which we can control the rules, a world in which we can set up rewards for good behavior, and punishments or penalties for bad behavior.

Think about it my friend! Think about any sport or athletic event imaginable. Every single one is about rewarding glory to those who perform well, and forcing shame on those who don't quite make it. Each sport has a series of rules and regulations that must be followed in order to properly win in this temporary perfect world. Here are some examples:

Basketball:
Dribbling a perfectly round ball down the court without stepping out of bounds and putting it through a round metal ring exactly ten feet above the floor, earns you two or three points. Pushing, slapping, shoving, exorbitant name-calling, or even chair throwing results in a foul and the other team is given a chance to prove their perfection. Due to the thunderous noise of the crowd, many times the coach must walk across the entire court just to congratulate a referee on catching his player's mistake, thank him for his vigilance, and even inquire about his splendid eyesight. Of course, all of this is done in the name of order and fairness.

Football:
Start out by correctly forming your team on the straight line of scrimmage. Next, hike the pigskin, which is by the way, no longer made from a pig but a perfectly shaped oval, synthetic ball. Execute the previously discussed plan of action, without diverting your course, stepping across the line of scrimmage early, or holding on to anyone else. Points and cheers go up for players who can correctly get the perfect little ball exactly 100 yards down field without stepping out of bounds. Extra points are even given if your skinny guy can kick it straight through two poles. If any one player gets too excited or dances around too much, he and his team are penalized for disrupting the normality of the game. Jeering boos and unfriendly comments are the result of not accomplishing these tasks. Even the friendly referees become less popular if the players make mistakes or errors. Interesting!

Bowling:
This one starts with a perfectly round ball and a pair of stylish shoes. Bowling alleys are so classy that they will not even allow you to bowl in common ordinary shoes. Next, ten pins are set up in perfect order and you get two chances to knock them all down. If you are skilled at this art, you can throw the perfect round ball down the perfectly straight path and knock down all ten pins on the first try. This game was created to prey upon the inadequate. If you don't throw a straight ball, you end up is what is cre-

atively called "the Gutter". Then you must stand there in your humiliation and stylish shoes as you wait an eternity for your ball to make its way back to you through a mysterious underground labyrinth and try for perfection once again. As if that were not enough shame, they then have a bar that comes down and knocks over all the remaining pins you missed mocking your futile attempts at the perfect score.

Consequently, if you look deep enough into any sport, you will find this human attempt at a perfectly controlled environment and a means of gaining and achieving this perfection through practice and hard work.

Are you surprised at this discovery? Are you bewildered to find that your favorite sport is no more than a futile attempt to capture a snapshot of this perfect life we are all striving to attain? Do we not also apply this to all aspects of our lives as well?

Our work, our schooling, our homes, our entertainment, even our weekends! In every aspect of our lives we feel if things are not going our way or that we are not doing as well as others, that something is wrong and that we are failing in some way.

I dare you right now to close this book and put it down without finishing this chapter! I double dare you!

However, due to the fact that you are currently reading this sentence is fact enough that even you have been brainwashed by our society and cannot leave things unfinished for fear of being a "quitter" or heaven forbid, "lazy!" So, my friend, I regret to inform you that there is little help I can offer you and wish you the best of luck in your many frazzled years ahead.

Gotcha!!

You know I could never leave one of my best readers to simply worry themselves into an early grave. I have good news! Great news in fact! Not only can you be free from the endless circle of searching for perfection in a world of mistakes and errors, but you can also help others escape this endless trauma of stress and heartache as well. All you have to do is **try harder!**

Sorry, I couldn't resist. Actually the opposite is true my friend. Remember back at the beginning of this horrendously long chapter, remember the cute little waitress coming up to your table and asking you, *"May I take your order?"* Ok, good. Now comes the hard part. Simply say, *"yes"*. Go ahead. Give it a whirl. *"y...y...yeah...yes"* Very Good! Now I want you look up from this book and say *"Yes, you may have my order!"* to the first person you see!

"Zwar you have completely lost it!" you are thinking? Yes I have, and know that it will never be returning to me! What is it that I have hopelessly lost? (Don't answer that by the way...) **It's my order!** I have completely and utterly lost any hope in ever becoming, creating, or accomplishing perfection in myself! And you know what, it feels great!

Do you know why? Because when you give up your hope for perfection or order, guess what you also must give up as well? You got it, stress, anxiety, pressure, worry, nervousness, trauma, hassle, fret, expectations, irritation, pessimism, exasperation, annoyance, aggravation, infuriation, negative thoughts, and did I mention stress?

Do you know what is the number one cause for all headaches, breakdowns, and panic attacks?

You guessed it, stress! All this junk and more gone from your life, and all it takes is the simple surrender of your order and hope for personal perfection.

Don't know where to start? Only you can answer that for yourself. What I would recommend however, is that you start with yourself! The best way to start is by failing. *"Oh my gosh, not that, anything but that!"* I am sorry to tell you my friend but the only way to truly break yourself away from the bonds of perfection is to completely and utterly fail! Attempt something that you know you cannot do. Try tap dancing, rock climbing, or cooking. Attempt something that will cause you to fall flat on your face in failure.

This may sound ridiculous or drastic, but I would like to offer this one last comment...

If you are willing to risk failure, I know without a doubt that you will not be alone in your failure. Not only will you find yourself being lifted up and dusted off by the countless others around you who have failed as well, but you will also see that in losing your order and perfection you have also gained a friend or two. Believe me when I tell you that one single imperfect friend is worth more than all the perfection and order you ever could have hoped to attain alone!

You will soon find that perfect order begins to lose its luster, and your dread and despair for failure and imperfection will fade away as well. You will even begin to laugh at your mistakes and the mistakes of others. What an amazing world this would be if everyone could take on great trials and difficulties with a simple smile and a friend.

So what are you waiting for, get out there and mess up big time!

May I Take your Order?

97 So I Have This Theory...

Chapter 7
Criminals of the Night

Anopheles quadrimaculatus, Wow! What a name! I took the liberty of asking three, non-partial, unrelated individuals what they believed this name represents. My findings were quite varied. Their responses included:

1. An evil, third century, Germanic Emperor
2. An intricately complex Anagram
3. A dreaded Lithuanian foot fungus

Whatever their verdict, they were all convinced that *Anopheles Quadrimaculatus* couldn't possibly describe something pleasant. Little did they know that their premature guesses were closer to the truth than one might think? This title is the scientific name for one of the most notorious and appalling insects this world has ever known. Its glossy stare and reverberating drone have been known to drive grown men to the point of insanity! With its razor sharp proboscis and insatiable thirst for our life giving liquid, this terror is none other than the blood-thirsty, six-legged vampire we so flippantly call the mosquito.

Now, I can hear you already, **"C'mon Zwar, a mosquito? Next chapter!"** Hold on a second, my faithful and yet slightly perturbed reader. Before you go and make the fatal mistake we humans have been guilty of making for centuries, allow me to explain to you my **Mosquito Theory**. It unveils not only the great mystery behind the mosquito, but also how you can take action against this plague on society as well.

> **Mosquito Theory:**
> The mosquito has used our sympathy for life to trick us into believing a lie. Mosquitoes, which are popular for their constant desire to drain us of our blood, do not actually require blood to survive.

First, let us discuss the animosity between ourselves, and these little creatures of doom. I think the answer to this is fairly straightforward.

We as humans are warm blooded; we need our blood to survive, and we feel pain and discomfort when it is taken from us. We become hostile when a creature with little to no morals or principals compromises any or all of these criteria.

Now I know many of you are foolishly rallying for the mosquito, the blood thirsty little devils of the night, by saying such things as:
"Hey, they gotta eat too," or
"I don't mind giving back to Mother Nature," or my personal favorite,

"They don't mean to hurt anyone, they are small and they do not understand." Oh that is just rich!

Why don't we just jump into the Amazon and wait until the Piranhas have had their fill, or feed our cat fluffy to the tiger at the zoo because he looks hungry and doesn't understand! Come on people, we must take a stand against this injustice. What we should truly be asking ourselves is why these little devils should be allowed to continue their abhorrent behavior, and what are they doing with all of our blood?

I believe that we can answer that question with another question. What does a mosquito eat when humans are not tramping around in the woods or wading through a swamp? Do the mosquitoes honestly believe that we will fall for the idea that they are getting all of their blood supply from squirrels, frogs, and pigeons? Are we supposed to believe that millions if not zillions of tiny little winged leeches can survive without a single drop of human blood? I would like to purpose to my readers an all Caps Lock *"YES!"*

Could it be that we have been had, duped, and bamboozled? Is it possible to consider for a moment the ridiculous idea that mosquitoes do not actually need blood to live their happy little ungrateful lives?

Did you know that a much more intellectual book than mine states that male mosquitoes do not bite or feed on blood, but munch on plant juices to sustain themselves? Plant juices! Mosquitoes are vegetarians? Very interesting.

So maybe we should draw our attention to the female mosquitoes. Why is it that these tiny she-vampires desire to harm us and steal our precious life blood? Apparently, female mosquitoes use our blood as a form of "baby formula" once they lay a batch of wriggling larvae eggs in a pool of water. I prefer to call it an addiction or an obsession. Some may call this behavior hereditary or second nature. Whatever you choose to call it, does not excuse the true crime behind this charade.

Let me put this another way. Do we see a stray dog tearing apart the trash and consider it a misunderstood gesture due to a lack of discipline in early adolescence? Do we view spaghetti noodles flung on the wall or ceiling as a youngster's attempts at expressing freedom of creativity? No. It's wrong because we have to clean it up or make it right. Have you ever had a mosquito make it right with you?

Have you ever had a little heart to heart with a single one of these tiny winged banshees, and if so, has she apologized and returned your stolen blood to you? No, of course not! They are clearly in the wrong and are continuing to cause us grief and misery, and for what? So they can give a little treat to their young ones at home? They are vegetarians! Get them started on the veggies!

Let me briefly explain to you the true hideousness of a single mosquito bite. It doesn't take a scientist with expensive equipment and a lab full of nerdy techies with pocket protectors to understand the process of a mosquito bite. In simple terms, the little buggers fly around until they spot a delicious human, land on said human, find any area of exposed skin, and commit the hideous crime by inserting their proboscis, a needle like straw-thingy, into the innocent person. Then, they calmly begin the process of extracting our life sustaining substance. Disgusting! Now, why does this process hurt and why does it itch afterwards?

Basically, when a mosquito injects her proboscis into one of our pores, she also injects just a touch of liquid that does not allow our blood to clot. She continues to inject this poison until she feels her craving has been fulfilled. However, similar to a pregnant woman undergoing midnight cravings, her veracious appetite is never quenched. This injection of poison is the initial pain that we feel. The anti-clotting agent is centralized, which is the cause for the slight lump or bump. The final stage, the itching and irritation are caused by the dilution of the poison throughout our blood stream... or something like that.

So in the end, after she's had her craving suppressed, this miniature she-devil flutters back home where she may enjoy a lovely dinner of leaves and sap with her loving husband. Never is he aware that his wife has been flying around committing hideous crimes, spreading disgusting germs, and giving the mosquito family name a terrible reputation.

"Oh my gosh Zwar, how long has this atrocity been going on?" you ask. Too long my friends, much too long. However, do not be too hard on yourselves. The circulation of knowledge and semi-truths is what this book is all about. Just be glad that you are now in the know. *"What can I possibly do to stop this crime against society?"* you wonder. Well my friend, stand up for your rights! Do not let yourself become another statistic in the great hoard of insect protectors and sympathizers. Let the multitudes of insect hippies around the world know how you feel about being violated again and again by those that they so ignorantly love and protect.

I say, *"no more!"* No longer shall we accept the she-mosquito's behavior as a slight irritation or necessary act of survival. Think of the little mosquito larvae. Do you think they like the rumors floating around the stagnate pond about their mother's questionable late night activities?

Again, what you do with this knowledge is completely up to you. But, I will say this, I for one am not going to allow my blood to simply fly away without a fight!

May we never forget that in helping just one misguided mosquito mother quit her addiction; we are helping an entire pool of happy, wriggling larvae.

107   So I Have This Theory...

Chapter 8
The Ancient Ages

Wow, the title of this theory sounds like a real winner! **The Ancient Ages** sounds more like a chapter heading out of my least favorite teenage pastime, History Class 4th period, more commonly known as "nap-time." However, before you doze off, or flip to the next chapter, know that my **Ancient Theory** is no bedtime story, and this little baby is far from heading toward a dusty bookshelf in the history section of any old library. Of course, I cannot give it away right at the beginning, but just be warned; this one delves deep into the very vapor of our past, and yet ties into the very fabric of our present day dilemmas. So, gather up all of your grey matter, and follow me. First, let's start with the theory:

> **Ancient Theory:**
> In the year 2450 B.C. certain events occurred which formed the world into what we know it as today. These events are all related, and their connections answer many of the mysteries of the ancient world we once thought unexplainable.

Intrigued? Let's dive in shall we? I feel that a good starting point is always at the beginning, so why don't we just take a look back shall we?

Let's say, oh, 6,080 years ago. What do we find here? Well, the only accurate account or documentation we have of this time period is none other than the Holy Bible. A splendid book the Bible is. It's historically accurate, without a single flaw or discrepancy, the oldest known text in the galaxy. Impressed? Did you expect less from the Creator of the Universe? I didn't think so. So, let's go way back to, let's say the year 4,075 B.C. What do we find here? Looks like the creation of the galaxies, solar systems, earth, plants, animals, and of course, the creation of humans.

Let's skip ahead, what do we find next? Looks like in the year 2,450 B.C. we had a pretty bad rainstorm, commonly known as the Flood. This Flood wiped out all known life on the planet except for those floating in a large boat. Then the creation of the rainbow is mentioned. After that, for some reason, the age of humans drops off dramatically, and we find that new continents have appeared.

Sounds quite different than the world we live in today, does it not? I mean, I haven't seen galaxies created in my lifetime, and the floods that we have now don't usually threaten all living things on the planet.

Why was this ancient world so different? I mean, we still live on the same earth, we still eat the same food, and we still walk, talk, and breathe just like they did back then right? How different could it possibly be?

Well, to be honest my friend, quite different indeed! However, for the sake of this chapter, we will focus on just a few points that I think you will find intriguing.

Let's start with this big bad rainstorm. Now I can already hear you whining, *"What's the big deal about a little rain? I mean it rained last week, and I don't think that 4,500 years from now anyone will care!"* Quite true my friend. What makes this storm such a doozy however, is that it had never rained before! Perhaps you think you may have misread that last little bit, so let me try it another way.

Before a crazy, old man named Noah built his little pleasure yacht and took it for a spin, no man had ever seen water fall from the sky! Genesis 2:5-6: "...For the Lord God had not sent rain upon the earth... but a mist used to rise from the earth and water the whole surface of the ground." - NASB

"Wait a second Zwar! No rain? I think you're mistaken." I am not my friend. However, I know what you are now thinking, no rain means no water, no water means no growth, and no growth means no life! Oddly enough, the Bible still says there was no rain. Let's just dig a little deeper shall we? We know that they got water from somewhere, perhaps streams or springs that arose mysteriously from the ground, but how did all the

plants get their water?

Well, let's take a look at the Bible's account of the event called the Flood. The entire story is quite fascinating, but I am extremely intrigued about the description of how the Flood started. This is what the textbook says: (Note: I have used three various translations to make sure we don't miss anything.)

Genesis 7:11-12
"... On the same day all the fountains of the great deep burst open, and the floodgates of the sky were opened. The rain fell upon the earth for forty days and forty nights" – NASB

"... That same day all the fountains of the great deep were broken up and burst forth, and the windows and floodgates of the heavens were opened. And it rained upon the earth forty days and forty nights." – Amplified Version

"... The same day were all the fountains of the great deep broken up, and the windows of heaven were opened. And the rain was upon the earth forty days and forty nights." - KJV

(Note: This is the first time the Bible speaks of the act of raining!)

Let me just do a little out-of-the-box thinking for a minute if you don't mind. These "windows" or "floodgates of heaven" must have surrounded the entire earth in a type of crystalline shell, or impervious ecosystem; something like a super greenhouse. When these "windows" or "floodgates" were intact, I believe that they allowed water vapor or some type of moisture to actually exist in or on the air itself. So that the plants themselves not only received the moisture they needed to survive, but thrived in this amazingly fertile environment. Sunlight itself was also different. Perhaps these windows acted as 100% UV protection and changed sunlight into a type of Miracle Grow!

I know that it sounds quite crazy all at once. However, don't think that I am going to just dump all of this on you and expect you to simply believe it without some sort of proof. Believe me, I have not merely made all of this stuff up, even though I must admit, it does sound quite like a lame science fiction novel. I believe that after I give you a few examples for each of these tall claims, you too will be scratching your beards in amazement.

Let's discuss a few defenses I have cooked up over the years. If this little theory of mine is actually true, then it explains a few tough questions. I'll just list them off before you lose all patience with me.

We have fossil records of gigantic plants and leaves that could never have grown in the atmospheric climate we now experience on the earth's surface.

Animals once existed that somehow just couldn't cut the mustard after the Flood. Dinosaurs for example, these giant beasts, most of which were plant eaters, may have had a hard time with the new limited and puny vegetation. Perhaps, it was the new extreme heat and harsh rays from the now unguarded sun that put them on the endangered species list.

Also, I would like to point out that the age of humans started to drop off dramatically after this point. Before the Flood, humans were living to the ripe old age of 600-800 years old. Now, if we make it to 100 we are living large! I would venture to say that this new environment affected our lifespan as well. I believe that the old atmosphere kept the human body from aging, and allowed them to reach far greater ages than our environment and ecosystem allow today. Perhaps organs we have no use for today, such as the appendix and tonsils, played a large role in our survival in that ancient world. But, enough about Biology and Zoology, let's take a gander at Astrology and Geography. (Remind you of your 6th grade class schedule?)

First, Astrology. "Smart-Guy-Scientist-One" says:

"We have conclusive proof that 150 billion years ago a large asteroid struck the earth, causing the entire earth to become shrouded in a cloud of dust cutting off all sunlight for an extremely long time, killing off all plants and large animals. This is what we believe killed off all of the dinosaurs, and led us into the Jurassic Period, in which only rats and cockroaches survived." (I may have paraphrased here and there, but you get the idea.)

Next, we have "Smart-Gal-Scientist-Two." She states:

"We have evidence of large craters on the earth's surface that indicate evidence of a number of large asteroids striking the earth. These impacts were enough to throw the earth on a wobble around its axis, causing the polar ice caps to melt, as well as numerous volcanic eruptions. This mixture of lava and ice led to an incredible shift in the earth's crust; moving the earth's tectonic plates away from each other and settling them where we know them today. Obviously this process took billions and billions, maybe even zillions of years and probably killed off all the dinosaurs, as well as, any other animals we scientists cannot explain." (I believe that was the exact quote she used.)

Lastly, we have "Bible-Thumping-Anti-Science-Guy." He states:

"Evolution is stupid. I didn't come from a monkey. God created everything. He even made the Flood, and it killed off all the dinosaurs. He didn't want them anymore. This asteroid and Pangaea talk is all horse manure. Where did all the water come from? God made it appear! Where did the dinosaurs go? God made them disappear! That's the problem with people these days, too many stupid questions!"

Well my friend, who is right? Scientist One? He's got a good point; a large asteroid would have completely changed the world's ecosystem. Scientist Two? She's got something going with the splitting up of the continents! How about the Anti-Science Guy? Does everything truly have an explanation? If neither can be proven, do you really want to have come from a monkey?

Again I ask you, which one is right? Are they all wrong? To tell you the truth my friend, I believe that to a certain extent, they are all correct. Why can't we use what we know from science, and apply it to what we know from the Bible? Do they contradict? I think not.

Without further ado, let me broaden your horizons for you! Go back to what we know is true from the Bible. We know that the earth was without rain, and we know that the "windows" or "floodgates of heaven" surrounded it. I would like to propose to you my friend that the world was also without oceans or lakes, but filled with these springs or mists that sprang up from the earth's crust from what the Bible calls, "the great deep". Take a water balloon for example; the outer layer simply floats over the liquid center.

Now, the Bible says the "floodgates" or "windows" of Heaven were opened. How do you think God opened them? A miracle? It's possible, but don't you find it far more marvelous that the Creator of the Heavens and Earth may have known when an asteroid was planned to strike the earth, and made provisions for it.

Once this asteroid or multiple asteroids broke through the "windows of heaven," I believe they then struck the thin crust surrounding the earth and broke it apart. This would explain the horrendous amounts of water coming up from under the earth as well. As a matter of fact, it would also explain the separation of a Pangaea mass of continents into what we have today.

My mind just races with example after example of geographical wonders that have baffled the human mind for centuries, such as, the Grand Canyon being carved out by terrific amounts of water pressure, and massive caves forming in instants of cataclysmic changes in water and earth.

Mountains, valleys, oceans, and lakes all being torn apart and placed gently where they rest today. It truly is astounding. It even explains how fossils of all species were formed due to tons of mud burying them all instantly.

I think the real kicker for me, which ties all of this mumbo jumbo into one, neat, little package, is the one promise that God gave to Noah after He had scrubbed the earth clean.

Genesis 9:13-15: "I set My bow in the cloud, and it shall be for a sign of a covenant between Me and the earth. It shall come about, when I bring a cloud over the earth, that the bow will be seen in the cloud. And I will remember My covenant, which is between Me and you and every living creature of all flesh; and never again shall the water become a flood to destroy all flesh." – NASB

Fantastic! A rainbow! He used the changed atmosphere and the changed sunlight as a promise that He would never again flood the earth. Again, I find it fantastic that he used something as simple as sunlight shining through water as it falls to the earth as a promise to us! Think about it, apparently Noah and his family had never before seen this phenomenon. Meaning that it had never rained, was cloudy, or that the old "windows of heaven" had previously changed the sunlight. Amazing!

So I am sorry to disappoint Scientist-One and Two, and even sorrier that I have to tell our friend the Bible-Thumper that those dang scientists are no longer the evil tools of Satan. But it looks like we are all looking to justify the same thing!

Asteroid... Flood... Continents... Dinosaurs... A completely new Ecosystem, they are all related. And it looks like they are all woven together in such a way that it once again points out that our wonderful Creator has everything under control and we are just along for the ride of our lives!

121   So I Have This Theory...

Chapter 9
Disgustingly Sanitary

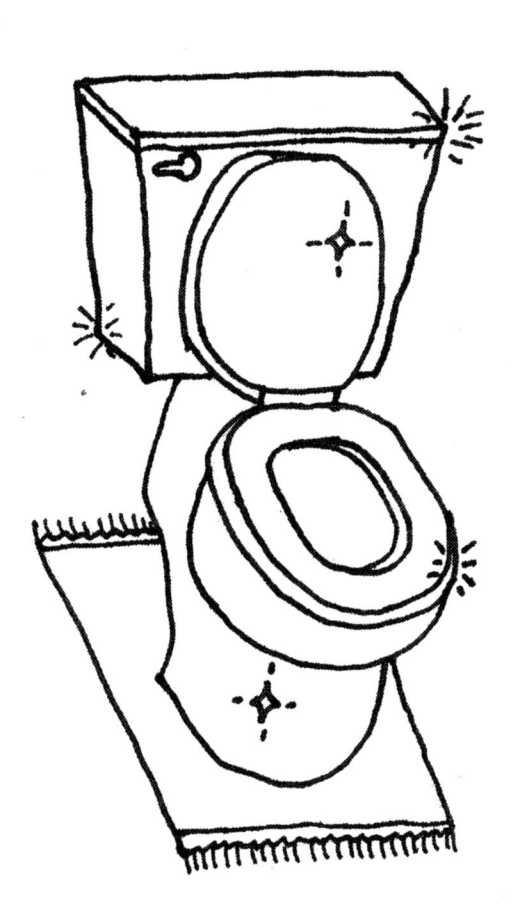

Here's a little something for you to ponder the next time you are waiting in line at a fast food restaurant or riding in an elevator. It's nothing really fancy; however, it is something that you will have a hard time forgetting. This theory is not for the squeamish at heart and I hope it doesn't make you change your living habits too drastically.

I do however, hope that it makes you stop and ponder, if only for a moment, about some of the odd things we humans do out of simple habit or routine. What I would like to focus on mainly is the reasoning or purpose behind each of these, oh; let's just call them "nuances" for now.

I've already promised that this one will be short so I won't draw out all the ugly details. Basically, I'll simply start with a few thoughts that may have flitted across your brain from time to time. Here are a few for starters:

"Make sure you wash your hands after you use the restroom!"

"That meal was great! I wonder if anyone has a stick of gum."

"Will that be cash or credit?"

"Just give me a call from the pay phone after the movie."

"I can't believe it's taking the doctor so long, I'll just read one of these magazines!"

"Hold on to the handrail honey."

"Can I use somebody's cell phone real quick?"

"Hold the elevator! Could you press the 6th floor for me?"

"Do you want to push the shopping cart for mommy?"

"Oh great! The roll of toilet paper just ran out!!!"

Now, I'll admit these thoughts seem pretty random, unconnected, and just plain bazaar. However, rest assured that they all have something in common. Can you spot the link? Hmm? Aright I'll drop a hint… check out the title of this theory. I call it my **Disgustingly Sanitary Theory**. Still got nothing? Allow me to enlighten you then.

> **Disgustingly Sanitary Theory:**
> **Humans that are concerned with sanitary cleanliness have a tendency to perform certain tasks out of habit or ignorance which they believe are aiding them in maintaining a pristine environment. However, many of these tasks are attaining quite opposite results.**

Basically this theory is simple. What I have found is that we humans seem to go to great lengths in our attempts at remaining incredibly clean.

Sanitary, pure, flawless, fresh, unmarked, new, unblemished, spotless, hygienic, pristine, immaculate, tidy, bright, perfect, and thousands of other ridiculous words that all lead back to the same sick obsession.

Honestly, I do not know why we are infatuated with this desire, but the key might be somewhere in my **Human Order Theory.**

However, what I would like to point out in this chapter is the amazingly bazaar things we do, thinking they will help us achieve perfect cleanliness, but are actually having disgustingly opposite affects. Let's break this down into simpler terms.

We as humans have adopted certain ideas and practices that we see as basic and cleanly exercises, but are, in actuality, bizarre, disgusting, and disturbing when you stop and think about the acts themselves!

So, just what are these nasty and ridiculous acts? I've already listed some of them above. "What are you talking about Zwar? I didn't understand those quotes the first time I read them!" you might ask, and rightly so. I understand that your mind may be trying to reject what I am telling you. True professionals, such as psychiatrists, may call this sort of thing denial. It is a tragic, yet quite common little disease. (Simply bear with your tender little mind and keep reassuring yourself that everything is going to be all right. The confusion should go away in a few hours, if not please put this book down and call a professional immediately!)

Let's process these examples one at a time shall we? Below are some of the disgustingly sanitary acts that we all have been involved in at one time or another. I am certain that there are many more, however, I don't want to overload you all at once. So, read them slowly and ponder each one with caution. Take as many breaks as you need. With that said, take a deep breath and we'll get started.

I would like to first talk about the act of washing the hands. Every grandmother's favorite chore, "Wash your hands before you eat!" Apparently, this act is believed to clean the dirt and bacteria from the hands so that they are not ingested while eating. Sounds like a good plan, but does it really work?

Sadly no, it could actually make things worse! Just think about it...

Johnny comes in from outside after playing in every mud puddle he could find. He is overcome with hunger as soon as his mom's amazing grilled cheese sandwiches hit his nostrils. "Go wash up," she says lovingly. Johnny runs into the bathroom, flips on the warm water, slaps the bar of soap, rinses, turns off the water, (and we'll give Johnny some credit here…) actually dries his little hands on the hand towel. Racing to the kitchen he devours two delicious sandwiches along with a few billion bacteria and other slimy particles.

"Wait a second Zwar! He washed his hands first; he couldn't have eaten any bacteria or slimies!" You exclaim. Oh really, are you so certain? Denial can be a nasty little habit.

Let's run through it in slow motion. Johnny **opens the door, turns on the faucet, wets his hands, soaps, rinses, and then ... OH NO... he touches the same faucet again!** Then he rubs the newly wetted nasties on the hand towel that so many others have done in the past, gaining new nasties. He then trots off to the kitchen leaving behind fermenting nasties on the faucet handle, hand towel, bathroom door, and of course yummy cheese sandwiches. Sick! Enjoy your lunch Johnny, you little sicko! I don't even have the stomach to explain to you what happens when Johnny washes up in a public rest room. Disturbing!

Let's next discuss the act of curing bad breath with chewing gum. After lunch, Johnny has the sensation that his breath may not smell terrific. (I know this never happens with little boys, but just humor me for now!) So what does Johnny decide to do? Bad breath, no problem, grown-ups just pop in a stick of gum. Perfect. So, following their example, he does the same. Bad breath solved, right? Well yes, and no. What also happens is that all the remainders of his cheese sandwich also join in with the breath curing gum as well. So, Johnny goes on his merry little way, chewing his minty fresh gum filled with pieces of toast and cheese for hours and hours. Disgusting!

How about the act of visiting the doctor's office? It's a hospital so it must be sanitary, right? Well, let's find out.

Later that day, Johnny has a doctor's appointment, nothing serious, just a little sniffle and mild cough. While waiting for the ill-tempered receptionist to call his name, he sits with his mommy and stares at the drab reception area. He spots some colorful toys in the corner and proceeds to play with them, while his mother flips through a few magazines.

Apparently, they are unaware that this is a hospital. Hospitals are where sick people go, constant sick people, coming and going, day after day. Oddly enough, these sick people play with the same colorful toys, flip through the same magazines, and cough, spit, sputter, sneeze, snot, and just plain nastify the same things that Johnny and his mommy have in their hands this very instant! Gross!

How about a trip to the movies, can't be too many germs or nasties there right?

Well, after the doctor's office, Johnny gets dropped off at the movies with his friends. (Johnny is very mature for his age, and he is in a safe neighborhood, so relax.) He is told to simply call when the movie is over and his loving mother will come pick him up. The movie gets out, the crowds disperse, and after a game of air hockey with pucks and mallets that haven't been cleaned since 1989, Johnny makes his way to the pay phone to call his mom. After popping in 35 cents, a quarter and a dime that have seen there share of sticky hands and pockets in their lifetime, a friendly voice answers and lovingly tells him she will be there in ten minutes.

Loving... my butt! I wonder if Johnny's mother is aware that there is no special sanitary task force that scours the city in search of contaminated pay phones that they can scrub down with disinfectant!

Actually, Johnny just put his ear and cheek up against a piece of plastic that kids, teenagers, adults, hobos, and circus carnies have been breathing on, touching, and basically rubbing on their faces for years and years and all she can say is, "Thanks for calling dear." Shameful!

I won't even get into Johnny's escapades at the arcade, petting zoo, playground, or library. Just know that any one of these places is nothing but a hot bed of bacteria simply waiting for a guest to drop by! I cannot finish this chapter without pointing out possibly the most disturbing nuance of all. I hesitate even mentioning it to you, simply to spare you the certain disgust in discovering the real truth behind this atrocity! However, I feel it is my duty to at least make this information available to you, what you do with this knowledge is entirely up to you my friend.

Here's the scenario.

Let's say, that it is a beautiful day in the park. You are there with your best friend, just laying out under a shade tree relaxing and staring up at the fluffy white clouds as they lazily float by overhead. You see another friend approaching and get up to meet her, taking in the beautiful green grass and swaying trees. Your friend happily greets you and is about to give you a loving hug when she points at a smelly brown substance on your arm. You notice the brown smudge, and recognize its pungent odor immediately. "I must have been lying where a dog relieved itself," you offer. "No matter," you reach in your pocket and pull out a few squares of tissue. Wadding up the tissue you smear the doggy doo off your arm and toss it in a nearby trash bin. As you both stroll away, you place your arm on your friend's shoulder and casually ask, "Well, where do you want to go for dinner?"

Do you see something wrong with this picture? You shouldn't, you do it almost every single day! Now before you start yelling, *"What? That is so not true! If I had poop on my arm there is no way I could just wipe it off with a tissue and be ok with that!"* Really? Then why do you do the exact same thing with your hindquarters? I guess my question is, if you would not simply wipe dooky off your arm and think that you are clean, why is it that you do exactly that with your own booty? Don't think about it too deeply, because trust me, the more you think about it, the more you will want to install a bidet in your own bathroom!

So what are we to do with all of this knowledge of the nastiness around us? Never touch anything? Live in constant fear of contamination?

Not a chance. I am merely imparting upon you the facts. We as humans have the natural tendency to do things merely out of habit, and until someone points out that what we are doing has no point or actually harms us more than helps us, we are doomed to continue these nuances for the rest of our lives.

    I am not telling you all of this disturbing information to ruin the way you eat a good grilled cheese sandwich or make you burn all of your toilet paper tissue. I am merely trying to help you consider your own crazy habits to help you reevaluate your thoughts on cleanliness and contamination prevention. Perhaps someday we will all have personal bubbles that will allow us to roll and play without a care in the world. Oh, happy day!

So I Have This Theory...

Chapter 10
Running Noses

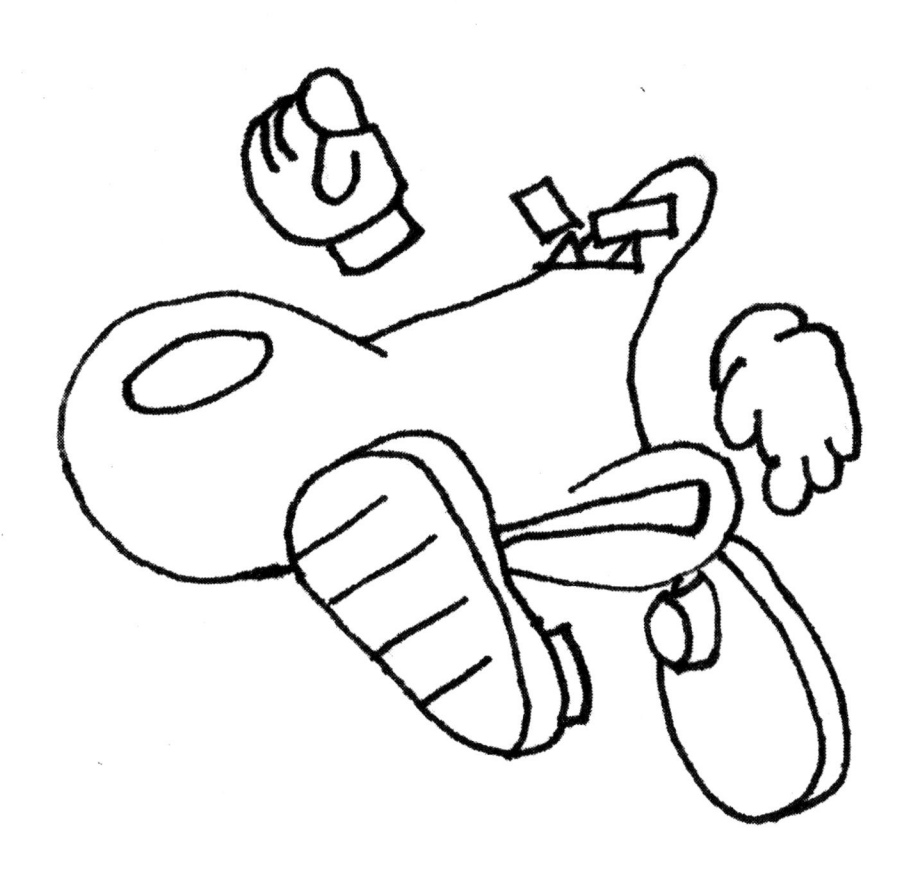

This one is a humdinger. I must admit, that even with the commanding schnauze with which I have been blessed, it was not I, who was so utterly befuddled by this nasal phenomenon, but a few of my brilliant friends and colleagues. They inquired about this common occurrence in a few passing questions. Before we get too involved, I feel that we should state their quandaries. The questions that so captivated me were stated something like this:

"Caleb, why is it that I get a stuffy nose when I go camping or when I am in a cold room?"

The second question was,

"Zwar, in the morning, why does my nose always run in the shower?"

No matter how hard I tried, I could not simply dismiss these enigmas, nor could I formulate a simple and basic solution for them. But never fear my faithful reader. It is a common fact that I do not give up easily. If my extremely limited resources cannot locate or formulate the answer to some of the world's most mysterious questions, then I will do my very best to confuse and exasperate any other ideas or theories in order to prove, beyond the shadow of a doubt, my utmost and upright solutions.

Therefore, imagine my utter joy and triumphant dance of glee when I finally arrived at the solution to these challenging and mind-boggling riddles. (Go ahead; imagine… ok enough, we have work to do.) This theory does take some thought, however the rewards to fully understanding this little beauty will prove to be knowledge beyond price.

First thing's first, we must agree on what we are discussing. It is simple enough. It starts with the innocent act of opening a window to "let a breeze in," or in the decision to get a little "fresh air." Sure, both of these ideas sound perfectly fine, and I am sure that at the time, a little cool breeze sounded like a good idea.

However, before you know it, you wake up at 4:00 a.m. because of your father's horrendous snoring, you realize you can't breathe through your nose, so you lay there until 6:30 a.m. just to hear your Aunt Gertrude hack up a lung in the bathroom and mutter something about a cold coming on.

I know exactly how you are feeling; we've all been there. But how could opening the window for a little fresh air be the cause of all of this grief? Perhaps, you are more common with the next scenario:

Your friends load up the car with as much luggage and soda as it will hold, and head off to the mountains for some "clean mountain air." Planning to simply enjoy some adventure and a few nights sleep. You all orient yourselves around the rocks and sticks jabbing you in your back and kill the last two remaining mosquitoes, (which have mysteriously found the one and only hole in your tent).

You wrap yourself tightly in your borrowed sleeping bag with only your nose protruding up from the mass of blankets and stocking caps. You are finally ready for your long awaited peaceful slumber. After about an hour of this blissful relaxation you notice that not only is everyone in the tent snoring louder than your Uncle Leroy after Thanksgiving dinner, but you also notice that your own nostrils are uncontrollably closing like your eyes during math class. It is at this time that you cannot help but ponder the thought,

"How did everyone else fall asleep before me?" *or maybe,* ***"What was that noise outside?"*** *but probably most importantly,* ***"Why is my nose all stuffy?"***

Well, I'm glad you asked! Not only do I have an amazing answer for this ongoing mystery, but I also have hope that the knowledge you will acquire in the learning of this phenomenon will help you to understand other questions that may be plaguing you at all hours of the day or night. The theory itself goes a little something like this:

> **Stuffy Nose Theory:**
> **Our noses become stuffy when we subject them to prolonged periods of tightly packed air. This blockage is relieved only when we increase the temperature of the particles, allowing them to depressurize and move freely.**

The key in understanding my **Stuffy Nose Theory** is to fully appreciate a few laws of chemistry and physics. Now, I know what you are thinking, "Whoa Zwar, I didn't buy a textbook you know." I can understand that some of you may be feeling a bit of apprehension toward the sciences, but again, understand that I am only slightly smarter than you, and I will break it down so even the simplest astrophysicist can appreciate its simplicity. Only two simple laws will be needed in order to follow along with this theory.

The first law is that hot air rises, thus cold air does not. Simple enough, right? The second law is that pressure, or tightly packed ma-

terial always seeks an area with less pressure or less material. Kindergarten stuff right?

First, let's discuss the easy one, hot air rises. I did not have numerous scientists work on this theory in the lab; however, if they had I would have had them perform two simple tests that you can do at home.

1) Go outside when it is Butt-Cold*, take a deep breath, and blow it out. Observe. Watch the warm air, or steam, from your lungs float up and rise until it dissipates.

2) Place a small paper bag over a heat source such as a stove or lamp without catching anything on fire, and observe it float or rise into the air. A mini air balloon.

Even with these basic experiments we can see that yes, heat rises and it does so without fail. This law, I am certain, has a fancy name along with the ingenious man who discovered it; however, I do not know it and am uninterested as to which smart man made its discovery. I am however, quite intrigued by the law itself, as it comes in quite handy in solving our stuffy nose mystery.

Next, we must discuss the idea of tightly packed particles and their

---

(* Butt-Cold: (a calculated temperature used by mathematicians and physicists around the world, approximately less than 23° F / -3° C))

desire to move to an area of less populated pressure. This thought is quite simple; as I am sure it has occurred to you on multiple occasions. To illuminate this idea more clearly, let me create a few scenarios for you.

The first takes place on a crowded street in New York City. *You are driving a fifteen-passenger van with twelve screaming kids in the back. It is 5:01 p.m. and you are late for their 4:30 p.m. soccer game. The streets are packed with cars and semi-trucks. You glance up at a billboard that reveals a serene image of a happy couple sitting on the beach under a palm tree with no one around as they sip some fruit juice. It is at that instant you nearly rear-end the car in front of you, slamming on the brakes you manage to spill little Timmy's soda all over one of the world's loudest junior goalies. You would do anything to be on that little beach far, far away from the traffic, noise, and soda covered goalies in your backseat.*

The second scenario can simply be demonstrated at night. *Start by wearing dark clothes and possibly a hat. Go to a nearby garage where cars may be found. Find a car with tires. (You will find that many come with tires included.) Try and chose a car you do not recognize as your own. Then, simply remove the protective cap from one of the tire stems, and press down on the air release mechanism. You should hear a slight hissing sound, hopefully no one else will. This sound is the high-pressured air* of *the tire escaping to the outside due to the drop in air pressure. You can repeat this exercise if needed, as long as you are not found or identified.*

Let's face it; none of us likes stress or pressure. We all want to escape to somewhere with less pressure or more freedom to move around. Try asking someone which they prefer better, a crowded subway or an open dance floor!

These thoughts, coupled with the simple fact that hot air rises, means that we are more than ready to tackle this nose theory head on.

Let me brief you quickly on what happens when you breathe through your nose. Your lungs expand to fill with air; this air is drawn through the nose or mouth. Once in the lungs, oxygen is separated from the air and is pushed back out through the nose or mouth. This simple process is repeated several hundred times per day.

Just like the air intake on any machine or automobile, our bodies also were made with a built in filtration system to separate particles and harmful agents from the air before it enters our lungs. The main filtration system is as plain as the nose on your face. (A little bit of wit never hurt anyone.) Your inner nose is covered with bunches of little gangly hairs. These hairs, as well as other filtration equipment in your nasal cavity, separate out all of the bad stuff that comes flying through on its way to the lungs, thus creating boogers.

When I was a child I was always amazed and curious as to the origin of my boogers, and what they were for, other than for flicking them at my sisters.

Now that we are all on the same page, we will discuss the difference between cold air and hot air. Believe it or not, cold air has a higher density than hot or warm air. Don't believe it? Allow me to explain by reviewing our previously determined laws. **Warm air rises and high pressure wants to move to low pressure.** I think it is fair to say that due to the pressure and crowding of the cold air the warm air moves out or perhaps is pushed out by the colder, more densely populated cold air. Confused? Perhaps, you can grasp it another way. Think of water. In its heated, vapor form it is free to float and fly anywhere it pleases. When the water temperature drops it is forced into a frozen rigid shape, locked in and tightly compacted. Air follows the same rules of nature. Because the warm air can rise and the cold air cannot, it simply sits on the bottom, all crowded, cranky, and compacted.

So, if we think back to our misfortunate campers or Aunt Gertrude and her nasal congestion, we may actually begin to tie together some loose ends. **Colder air is denser than normal warm air.** Meaning, that it is more tightly packed with each other, and just like any gang or mob they simply cannot stay clean or resist making a mess. So what happens to our poor noses when they are forced to clean and filter through this overabundance of crammed, cold air? It simply cannot take the overload of filth.

It tries it's best to create boogers on a normal basis in order to clear out all the bad particles, but it cannot keep up with the massive attack of dense, cold air.

This overabundance is forced to flood back into the nasal area and continues to back up until total shut down it inevitable. After you understand this principal of densely packed cold air, answering the second question is a breeze. Remember what it was? It's ok, my memory doesn't work either, it was:

"Zwar, in the morning, why does my nose always run in the shower?" I can hear the gears turning in that tiny little mind of yours. Allow me to assist you.

Basically, after a cool night's sleep, when your overwhelmed nose is treated to warm air in say, the shower or physical exercise, the high-pressured cold simply flows out seeking a place of lower pressure and less crowded surroundings. Thus, causing your nose to run and make you snot all over the place. Isn't that great!

So from now on my friends, if you find yourself congested and unable to get a good nights rest, or are in need of a cool breeze but afraid of waking up in the morning all stuffy and snotty. Fear not, you need only to get up and warm those nasal particles with a brief jog or a warm shower. Before you know it, your nasal passages will be free and clear, and you can settle back down for that long winters nap. The next time you feel that little sniffle coming on, don't just run for the tissue, keep running! Get those particles warmed up so they simply flow right out. Give your nose a break, and try not to blow it!

So I Have This Theory...

Chapter 11
Dragons

What thoughts are triggered in your mind at the mention of dragons? Long lost days of knights, horses, and castles? Stories told of maidens in despair and heart pounding duels? Tales with swords clashing, armor flashing, and legendary heroes born overnight? Bedtime dreams filled with regal knights who rescue princesses from enchanted castles and narrowly escape fearsome fire-breathing dragons?

We can each think of a dozen stories we have seen or heard about these wonderful creatures, but do we really know where these fantastic stories originate?

We have historic proof of knights and their valiant escapades. We even have replicas of the armor they wore into battle. We have royal family lineage that can be traced back through history to the ancient kings and queens of old. We have poetry handed down through the ages of glorious battles and scandalous love stories. We have actual weapons and castles created in a time long before our own. We have scales of ancient dragons and scorch marks from their deadly toxic breath. We have untold amounts of...

"Wait a second! We don't have any scales of dragons or burn marks from their scathing breath. Come to think of it, we don't have any proof whatsoever that dragons ever existed."

What's going on here? No dragons? No green, scaly monsters with enormous, leathery wings and flaming nostrils of death? How can this be? What about all the stories and pictures, what about Puff?

Let's get some things straight here. First off, I don't care what you may have heard from little Jackie Paper, Puff was not a real dragon. Even if he did make a catchy tune in the 60's, he remains on the fictional list.

Now that we have that settled, let us first distinguish or categorize these mysterious mythological animals. I believe it is only fair to give Webster a fair shot at it, after all; his book is much thicker than mine!

Drag'on: (drag'ęn) *n.* a fabulous fire-breathing serpentine animal of great size and fierceness.

Neat-o, or should I say, fabulous! So, a serpentine, fire breathing, fierceness all wrapped up in one critter, sounds like a fairly good definition. Let's give Oxford a try.

Dragon: *n.* a mythical monster like a giant reptile, able to breathe out fire. ORIGIN – Greek drakōn 'serpent'.

Well, now, this one is interesting! A giant reptile whose name originated from the word, "serpent." That's twice now our scaly friend here has been called a giant serpent like creature. I wonder if a dragon would take offense to these descriptions? Now that we have a few reasonable definitions to go by, let us continue our hypothesis.

Dragons were obviously feared creatures back in a day of mythology and superstition. Even to this day, they remain objects of fascination with us humans. From movies like *"Reign of Fire," "Dragon Wars," or "Shrek"* to television commercials such as *"Geico Direct"*. We love writing about them also, *"Lord of the Rings," "Eragon," or "Harry Potter,"* to name a few. Let's face it; we humans are completely obsessed with dragons, no matter the size, color, or character of the beast. Yet, if these creatures never existed, from what did we create them, and why are we so fascinated with them now?

I would like to propose to you inexplicable and yet indisputable evidence to the true existence of dragons.

Rest assured that yes, dragons did exist and quite possibly still do exist in certain areas of the world today; however, they may not exist in quite the way you might expect.

If your mind is filled with skepticism and excitement at this very notion, then sit back and hold on tight for the mental ride of your life, my friend. As my **Dragon Theory** unfolds, you will begin to understand the many long kept secrets surrounding the mysteries of dragons and their true existence. The most startling aspect however, is the connection I have uncovered between the history of the dragons and our own history as humans.

Let us first take a look at the history of the dragon itself. This history is a bit shaky due to the lack of physical evidence we have accumulated over the years. However, what we can piece together from legends and otherwise non-trustworthy sources are a limited number of what I like to call, *"Dragon Facts."* These *"Dragon Facts,"* will allow us to piece together a glimpse of these ancient beasts so that we may better understand and appreciate them. (Luckily, since they are already *"Facts,"* we know they do not need to be scientifically proven further!)

Dragon Fact #1: *Dragons live incredibly long lives.*
Example: *"The Hobbit"*: Smaug, the dragon of the Lonely Mountain, out lived three dwarf generations!

Dragon Fact #2: *Dragons scare humans and do occasionally eat them.*
Example: Homestarrunner.com: Trogdor the dragon loves "burninating" the villages and peasants!

Dragon Fact #3: *Dragons have large teeth and scales.*
Example: *"Godzilla vs. Mothra"*: Mothra had no chance!

Amazing, I feel like I know more about dragons already! They are like the uncle that is never around, but everyone has tons of stories about. Now we have a standard we can use when verifying what a dragon is and what a dragon is not. So, what is our next step? Well, since we have such a fascination with them, let's see if dragons could blend well with humans.

I could see how dragons would be an awesome addition to any backyard barbeque. You might respond with, "What if he burns down the house and the deck, along with all the burgers?" Good point, hmm… well, I am sure that a dragon would be a great snowplow! Again you might inquire, "What if he hits a car or incinerates all the mailboxes?" Touché my friend, touché! Well, you can't argue that a dragon wouldn't make an excellent guard dog. "Until he eats the mailman," you retort. You know, I think you might be right.

Dragons and humans simply would not coexist well with one another. Too much drama and no one likes that. So let's recap. Dragons live long lives and scare humans with their long teeth and scales, therefore humans and dragons would not make good neighbors. Sounds about right to me, let's make a cool bullet list so this looks more professional.

- **Dragons seem to exist only in our stories or imaginations.**
- **We seem to have no physical proof of the existence of dragons.**
- **We seem to be strangely attracted to the thought of dragons.**
- **We as humans want nothing to do with a real live dragon.**

Confused? Don't worry, we are closer to discovering the truth behind dragons than you may think. Let us now discuss our strange human reaction toward dragons. In doing so you might be surprised to learn more about humans than about dragons. "What the heck is that suppose to mean Zwar?" Do not get lost in a bit of friendly wordplay my auspicious and yet easily excitable reader; simply continue reading.

What is it that we humans do when we find something we dislike or find distasteful? I believe the answer could be a number of things, so let me clarify with everyone's favorite, a scenario.

Let's say little Susie is washing dishes. Precious little brother Bobby slithers into the kitchen with a small object clutched in his dirty little hands. Without a sound Bobby ever so gently places his newly found grasshopper friend on his sister's shoulder. Much to Bobby's delight his sister reacts exactly as anticipated. With an ear shattering screech in which only little girls are qualified, Susie announces to her brother, mother, and next door neighbor her great distaste for this innocent gift from her brother. In one motion Susie is able to obliterate the grasshopper with the frying pan while throwing dishwater and utensils at her beloved brother.

Now, let us look to our unfortunate friend the grasshopper. How did his role in this short exchange merit such a dramatic exit? Do you think precious little Susie feels even a twinge of remorse for this brutal fatality? Was Susie ever in any danger at all? I believe that these three questions are sufficient enough to answer all of our quandaries regarding dragons and their existence.

Let us imagine for a moment what would happen if a dragon waltzed into town looking for a drink and a friend… Would the people of that town welcome it with open arms and buy it a drink? Hardly! I believe they would give it more of a Godzilla greeting. Whip out the tanks and guns! Kill the Beast! Don't let it escape!

Now, where does this come from? The dragon was just thirsty and lonely. "Kill it! Squash it with a frying pan," Susie would squeal.

Shocked? Perhaps, you shouldn't be. Let's just say the people of that town did succeed in obliterating the poor, lonely dragon. Would they feel sorry for what they had done? Would they apologize to the dragon's family and friends? Fat chance! They would celebrate, take pictures with the dead creature, and tell stories for years to come of how they single handedly saved the town by destroying the fearsome dreaded beast. Interesting.

Lastly, let us look at the concept of danger. Was Susie or any of the townies ever in any real danger? This is where it gets tricky. To Susie, this disgusting insect was in violation of multiple atrocities and needed to be exterminated. To the townies, they naively believed they were in real danger of losing their homes and their lives from this menacing monster. Yet, were they really? With this thought, let us regress to the original story.

Remember the medieval knights on the white steeds traveling to far off lands to slay the dragon that had been menacing village peasants and hoarding treasure? The legends of glorious battles, stories of villages saved, miraculous escapes and near misses, all revolving around these "terrible" monsters we call dragons. Sound familiar? Well, one crucial role has yet to be filled. If it is true that the knights and village people were running around killing creatures and making up glorious stories, what were they killing?

Grasshoppers don't make for very convincing legends of valor; it had to be something much larger, much more frightening and mysterious! The answer is so obvious, and yet so disturbing. Dinosaurs! My **Dragon Theory** will spell it out more plainly for those of you who seem to lack even a portion of creative thought:

> **Dragon Theory:**
> **In the Dark Ages, medieval knights and villagers killed off the remaining helpless dinosaurs simply out of fear and confusion then created stories of dragons and fire-breathing monsters.**

Since those devious and dark ages, we have wondered two things. Where did all the dinosaurs go and how did we come up with these fantastic stories of dragons? If you have read my **Ancient Ages Theory**, then naturally you already know what happened to the majority of the dinosaurs. However, what happened to the rest? C'mon Sherlock, this one has "cover-up" written all over it. Isn't it obvious?

The knights needed to impress the ladies, so they would ride out, find some plant-munching dinosaur, and murder the poor crea-

ture only to bring back a few remains and a tall tale. Scandalous!

Oh, what valor, what honor! And you my friend have been swindled into believing this disgusting trickery for centuries. Enough is enough! No longer will we hide in our laboratories and cover up the truth, weaving tales of asteroids, dust particles, and ice ages to cover up the death of the dinosaurs. Stop breeding lies and besmirching the good name of the dinosaur! May we own up to our own folly and apologize to the world and the reptile kingdom. We cannot undo the past, but we can change the future. For starters, we must learn to embrace our scaly friends!

So hug an iguana, wink at an alligator, or high-five a python!

Perhaps, if we come to terms with our mistakes and try to make it up to our past enemies as the Bible instructs, "Love your enemy," we may yet have hope for the future. Who knows, maybe the dinosaurs have simply gone into hiding. They might come out if they know we really do love them and are not going to kill them on sight. Let us change the future for generations to come. Give up your narrow view of a giant, fire-breathing, smelly dragon. Embrace the warm, cuddly feeling you get when you think of a diplodocus, mastodon, or vilociraptor. I am confident that all we need is a little further understanding of each others personal space, and we can all live together in harmony!

So I Have This Theory...

Chapter 12
Chocolatey Fudge Pop

How many times has something like this occurred?

Little Jimmy does his very best to be a good boy all day while his mother is at the hair salon. He sits quietly, blankly staring at a magazine article entitled, "How to Lose Ten Pounds and Feel Great Doing It." Meanwhile, his mind keeps replaying his mother's words, **"Now Jimmy, behave yourself and be a good little boy while mommy gets her hair done and you'll get a little treat when we get home."**

Oh splendor of splendors! He can already taste this sweet reward of chocolate and fudge swirled to perfection in a brilliant masterpiece of ice-creamy delightfulness!

He jumps as he sees his mother's chair swivel and she smiles at him comfortingly, only to have his hopes dashed as she is directed into the brain wave scanner to have her mind scanned by that curious humming head device. After what seems like two years, the lady with the big teeth lifts the scanner and to Jimmy's dismay places his mother back into the chair by the mirrors.

He slowly sways back and forth next to the gigantic candy jar as his mother and Big-Teeth-Lady continue their endless code talk about manicures, revitalizing conditioners, and hip replacement surgeries. Finally, with a pat on the head and a "see you next month," from Big-Teeth, Jimmy tears out the door and heads straight for the car. Only the drive home now separates him from true joy and chocolatey happiness.

Jimmy already has his seat belt on, door locked, and window rolled down before his mother even places her purse on the seat. He now waits in agony as she pricks and prods her new creation in the mirror and mutters,

"Oh, she took too much off the front… What do you think Jimmy?"
Right on cue he responds as he has been taught, "You look pretty Mom, let's go home!"

With a smile from his mother he knows his last comment has sealed the deal and that his ice-cream promise is as good as gold.

As soon as the front wheels touch the driveway Jimmy is already out of the car and running for the front door. His mother calls something over his shoulder as he flings open the door, tosses his shoes in the corner, and slides to a stop in front of the refrigerator, all in one fluid motion. Flinging open the freezer, he reaches into the secretly stashed box of chocolaty-fudge-pops. Tearing off the wrapper and tossing it into the sink he plunges it into his mouth, enjoying every last flavorful moment. Biting off a chunk, he climbs the steps to his room.

All at once he is halted in this moment of ecstasy, his head seems under attack from space invaders. **Pound, Pound, Pound... moments turn into light years as he prepares himself for the worst. Just when he thinks he's finished, everything returns, his room, his mess, his ice-creamy delight. "Oh well," he shrugs as he bites off round two.** *Only to find this horrendous pain return to plague his noggin, again forcing him to hold his head in agony until the stinging slowly subsides.*

- What is this ridiculous phenomenon that can turn little Jimmy's happiest experiences sour in a matter of seconds?
- How could the one thing that he had been waiting for all day bring him such upsetting pain and confusion?
- Why do we know so little about something so simple?
- Where can I get a chocolatey-fudge-pop?

These are the kinds of questions that plagued me day and night until I arrived at this stunning conclusion.

I know that you are familiar with the phenomenon in which I am describing. I am also aware that you may have experienced the painful effects of this enigma yourself. Well, rest assured my good reader that my **Brain Freeze Theory** not only puts to rest the hidden facts behind this sickening experience, it also opens the floodgates to even more ridiculous thoughts as well. So sit back, relax, and leave the theorizing to me!

> **Brain Freeze Theory:**
> **When a cold substance is introduced to the throat and esophagus, it causes the constriction of blood flow to the brain. Proper precautions can be taken to eliminate these effects all together.**

First, let's lay some groundwork with a simple explanation of what is going on upstairs. I am proud to announce that the pain you feel after inhaling a cold treat too quickly is not tiny frost pixies hammering away on your central nervous system. **(I once interviewed a frost pixie, and he made it quite clear that frost pixies go nowhere near the human head nor do they enjoy hammering away on someone's cranial lobe. Actually he was pretty upset with me for even insinuating that he played a part in this heinous crime.)** So that's a relief, don't you think?

It's actually fairly complicated and somewhat scientific, so hooray for all those nerds out there who like the scientific mumbo jumbo. The actual process starts with the introduction of a cold substance into the oral cavity of the subject in question. (That would be the mouth for those who slept through "Anatomy and Physiology" 5th period.) Upon swallowing the cold substance, it then travels down the esophagus and into the stomach. Quite simple after all!

The problem occurs when the cold substance is pressed against the back of the throat and travels down the esophagus. This area also contains a very important artery called the carotid artery. What does this artery do? Well to be quite honest, for some of us, not much, for others this artery is the major pipeline that supplies blood and oxygen to the brain and allows it to function.

I can already see some of the light bulbs beginning to flicker in those of you who actually use your noggin for something other than a hat rack. To those of you who are not so inclined; the pain that we feel is none other than ice-cold blood flowing into our brain, but that is not all.

Nature has built in a safety mechanism. When something gets cold it tends to huddle up or constrict; to keep the warmth in. Our brain follows the same rule of nature. When it is attacked with a blast of cold blood it also constricts and huddles up to keep the cold out and the warm in. Thus your carotid artery also constricts and tightens to try and minimize the amount of cold.

This would be great, except for those of us who like our brains in a functional state. What happens when these arteries tighten up? Well, the blood flow and oxygen supply to our brain also closes up and instantly our brain is thrown into a state of starvation and deprivation. Sound too harsh for a simple ice-cream cone? It's really not if you think about it.

What is the common and accepted cure for a brain freeze? Simple, stop eating! **Have you ever wondered why once you stop swallowing the headache continues on for a few more aggravating seconds?**

You stop, yet it lingers there, torturing you and stealing the very joy out of your yummy treat. Why? Well, it takes time for your blood to warm, thus allowing your carotid artery to relax and let the blood flow freely throughout your noggin once again.

I know that you are now dying to know what you can possibly do to properly enjoy your favorite icy treats again. Believe it or not there is a way around this crazy brain freeze conundrum. Intrigued? First off, I feel that I must mention the fact that you can of course do what all boring people do and eat your yummy ice-cream treats very slowly to avoid too much cold all at once. If this is your style, go ahead and continue your mild enjoyment of life's simplest pleasures, as well as life itself for that matter. For those of you who grab life by the horns and want to make every minute count, I would like to offer a few other suggestions.

Remember that we are dealing with extremely cold temperatures flowing through our bodies that are made to operate at a constant 98.6°

F; quite far from freezing I am afraid. So our favorite frosty goodies, which hover around the 15-20° F range, are a bit of a shocker to our bodies. Don't lose hope however. What I would like to suggest to you are a few untested and mildly proven facts about how to rapidly consume your favorite chilled goodies and still come out smiling.

First and foremost, I cannot stress the importance of the proper protection. A heavy scarf is always a good idea before attacking any type of frozen dessert. Wrap the scarf tightly around the neck and throat region. A warm hat is also a fabulous idea. Be sure to cover all of the exposed regions (throat, neck, and forehead,) these are a few of the vital areas and are extremely susceptible to foreign cold material. These precautionary steps will aid the main affected areas directly, and help keep essential passageways clear and unobstructed.

Next, I recommend that you enjoy your frozen little snackeroo in similar temperature climates. In other words, allow your body to lower its own threshold of tolerable temperatures by getting it used to the cold externally. This will allow your body to readily accept the cold substance internally as well.

Think about it. Of course your body is going to have an adverse reaction when you put something frozen in it when its 85° F and sunny outside! What did you expect? Try a single scoop in December when there is a half a foot of snow on the ground and a wind chill of −15° F!

I'll bet you can gobble that ice cream down faster than a tubby kid puts away a Twinkie, without even the hint of a brain freeze!

Surprised? You most certainly should not be.

Why do you think everyone likes to sleep when it's a little chilly?
Why do you think coffee and tea are served hot?
Why did you take a hot shower this morning?

I could be getting a bit ahead of myself, but if you have been paying attention you should be able to spot the pattern emerging. Nothing? Hmm… allow me then to enlighten you on this one last point.

Cold is not some mystical, unknown thing. It is merely the absence of warmth. Warmth allows for motion. Warmth also happens to be a by-product of motion. It would be fair to say then that this warmth or heat is the presence of motion or energy itself. *"What are you getting at Zwar with all this technical jargon?"* you ask.

Just this, if heat or warmth is the presence of motion or energy, then cold is the absence of motion or energy.

Thus, when you suddenly introduce a substance into your body that has little to no energy, it floods throughout your system, shutting down and temporarily paralyzing all it comes in contact with. The opposite is true when you take a swig of hot coffee or tea. Yes, the caffeine has a small affect, but the true eye opener is the heat of the liquid itself.

The same is true with exterior conditions. Sleeping in a cold or chilly environment is conducive to a good nights rest because the cool temperatures slow the body itself. How many of you have found it difficult to drop off to sleep when it is hot and muggy in your bedroom? When we wake up what is it that really gets us going? None other than a hot shower and a steaming cup of java! I rest my case.

So, what can we derive from this endless bank of knowledge? I think the answer is quite clear. A proper understanding always leads to correct decision-making. With this new knowledge you can now understand and appreciate the affects of heat and cold upon your body and mind. You can now also see the hidden relationship behind energy and motion, as well as their common denominator; temperature. More importantly, you can now sit down outside in the snow with your hat and scarf wrapped tightly around you as you enjoy your favorite chocolatey fudge pop as fast as your little brain desires, and without a care in the world! Enjoy world! Enjoy little Jimmy! Enjoy tiny frost pixies!

So I Have This Theory...

Chapter 13
A Fishy Tale

Ah yes, everyone's favorite, the happy little fishes. They swim around their brilliantly colored lagoon of plastic plants and tiny sunken ships. They flaunt their superbly ornate oranges and blues only seen in their underwater world of tranquility; beauty so stunning it demands any passerby to pause in wonder and awe at their delicate splendor.

Lost in a trance at their slippery magnificence, many find themselves enraptured in the act of attempting to simply touch one of these underwater flowers, only to find themselves tapping on the glass uttering such words as "*here fishy, fishy*" or "*wake up fishy, wake up!*" Owners of these glass cases of heaven cannot resist but to stare at these scaly little angels as they dart and flit about their watery enclosures.

Time and time again owners find themselves racing home just to flip on the light and toss several bits of flaky food into the water. Then, hearts simply soar as their little gilled friends display their overwhelming loveliness as they dash here and there absorbing every last morsel. We are simply mesmerized not only by their beauty, but also by their activity.

They never seem to stay in one place, they are always moving, floating, hovering, or skimming around in the water. Wait a second… they are, aren't they? I mean, I don't think I have ever seen a fish stand or swim still.

Except for those droopy purple fish that are hard to tell if they are alive or dead. Other than those unfortunate boring fish, real fish never seem to stop moving, but how can that be? Don't the little beauties ever get tired? Don't they ever need to sleep? Sure, I know what most of you are saying, *"They sleep at night Zwar,"* or *"I've seen Finding Nemo and I know that fishes sleep."*

Not to dash your dreams or thoughts on certain movies, but I have personally snuck up on the fish in my aquarium at night and have always seen them slowly skimming around the tank.

Let's not forget the sport of night fishing. This activity is self explanatory, but for the few readers of mine who don't get out too often; night fishing is simply the sport where a fisherman goes out at night and catches fish using glowing lights, lures and lanterns. Now how could any of these nocturnal fishermen ever catch anything if the fish were asleep in their little fishy beds?

Some of you may now be arguing, *"Fishes can swim while they sleep"* or *"Sleep walkers can walk in their sleep, so sleep fishers can fish in their sleep…"* or something like that. Well, I would like to state that this idea is preposterous and I have no reason to reject or demote this hypothesis, so let's just move forward, shall we? You then might try and protect your dignity by saying, *"Maybe they just close their little fishy eyes and catch a nap here and there."* Now you're thinking! Of course, you are not completely correct, only I can be completely correct in my book, but you are very close.

I am sorry to report that fish do not have eyelids to close. Therefore, they cannot simply catch a bit of shut-eye because they cannot shut their eyes. You may find this hard to accept at first, so I will give you a moment...

...

...

...

Ok, now that you have had some time to reflect, we can now get back to business, namely, little fishy naps. Just because they don't have eyelids doesn't mean they cannot take little cat naps. Oops, I mean fishy naps here and there. So, problem solved right, end of story. Not so fast. We're just getting started. Let's take a deeper look at this nap idea.

A fish's nap probably lasts from five to twenty seconds maximum. I guess if a fish squeezed in enough of these tiny little naps, then it might obtain the rest it needs. However, there must be some type of drawback. Oh, rest assured my good reader, there is!

There is no need to fear however, comfort yourselves in knowing that my **Fish Theory** will be able to answer all of your questions regarding fish napping and much, much more. This theory will provide an answer to many of the uncertainties that surround our little fishy friends and allow you to better appreciate their circumstances. What is this little nugget of knowledge that carries so many joyful answers?

> **Fish Theory:**
> **Fish do not sleep as we do; they catch short naps between their darting movements. These delicate sleep patterns, if compromised, can have terrible repercussions on their energy levels, memory capacities, and thought processes.**

So that you may understand this brilliance correctly, we must first take a look at the adverse effects that lack of normal sleep has on our own bodies as humans. If we humans don't get enough shut eye, the first thing we notice is that our energy levels suffer, then we become forgetful, and if prolonged lack of sleep remains our reasoning begins to fail us as well. These effects are similar in the fish's realm as well. Let's dissect these effects so that we may better understand and appreciate the fish's point of view.

First, let's look at the lull in energy level. Now before you argue, *"Wait a second, fish have energy, they are always happily floating around my fish tank!"* Let's think about this deeper.

Are they, "happily floating around", or are they sporadically darting from one area of cover to another, in hope of catching just one more speck of slumber? Could it be that our happy picture of their endless gliding from one side of the aquarium to the other is merely a mindless cycle for these slippery little insomniacs and their hunt for a better life?

Oh sure, they swim about as we imagine them with smiles on their little, fishy faces, just happy to be alive. They cannot smile or frown however, they are doomed to simply swim, and swim, and swim.

The next ill effect from lack of sleep is forgetfulness. After our energy leaves us, and we do not replenish ourselves with sleep, the next thing that goes is our memory. As a student, they say the best thing to do during studying is to get plenty of sleep so that your mind can replenish itself and store all that you have learned. Deep, memory storing sleep is called REM sleep. Without this REM sleep, it is basically impossible to remember anything on a day-to-day basis. I would also venture to say that if sleep was not acquired over a period of time, moments would begin to blend together and any form of long-term memory would disappear completely.

My friend, we'll just call him Ryan, once cleverly pointed out to me that fish in an aquarium never seem to get tired of structures that are placed in their underwater world of plastic wonder. Say a castle for instance.

A fish will swim to one end of his little world, turn around and exclaim, *"A castle!"* swim in, around, and out only to turn again and discover, *"A castle!"* This cheerful little creature may be happy with this simple gift the rest of his life. Should we be happy for him?

Let us look at this from a different angle. Feeding time; the major bonding time when we humans interact with our wonderful pets. The only thing we have to worry about is over feeding them. *"Why? How could over feeding them be a problem? Wouldn't they just stop eating,"* you might ask.

Could you imagine Billy running home after a hard day in the sixth grade, tossing his books and muddy shoes on the carpet as he exclaims, "Mom, I'm hungry, and what are you going to do about it?" After barging into the kitchen, he finds his loving mother placing a steaming plate of food at the table. He scrambles up into his favorite chair and grabs his fork ready to dive into the three noodles of macaroni and cheese and one green bean. "What's this?" he exclaims. "I'm hungry!" "Oh, I don't want to over feed you dear," his mother gently pats him on the head and goes to make a phone call.

Well, I'll tell you right now little Billy would be upset city with three noodles and one green bean. I think you would agree that no mother would do this to her son. But, if we are not concerned about over feeding those we care for deeply, why care if we over feed our fish?

If you have been paying attention, you already know the answer. Fish have incredibly terrible short-term memories due to their lack of sleep. Therefore, they cannot even remember if they have eaten. We toss some food in and forget about it, but it is not so simple for them. *"Food!"* they exclaim, munch, munch, munch! Only to turn and discover, *"Food!"* munch, munch, munch.

This endless cycle of overindulgence could continue down a dangerous path. They could eat and eat until they are full, forget they have eaten at all, and continue to eat and eat until they are literally stuffed. Then its bellies up for little "Nemo" as he gets an all expenses paid trip on the porcelain express!

The final thing to go with complete lack of sleep is rationale itself. (This section of the book may prove to be somewhat disturbing to younger audiences and should be overlooked if uneasiness arises among you.)

For you to fully believe and appreciate what I am about to tell you requires you to have previously observed our little fishy friends for a period of time. What you may have observed is an act that is as disturbing in the fish's world as it is in our own. However, due to their lack of reasoning it has become a sad reality. It occurs as the little forgetful fish swim around in their tank, after a good meal of freeze-dried shrimp and flake food; they, like all animals, proceed to relieve themselves.

As this substance floats its way down to the pebbles, these delusional critters have been known to ingest portions of their own refuse. I can hear you already, "Sick! They eat their own poo!" Believe me; if these poor little sleep-deprived fish knew what they were doing they would be even more disturbed than you. They cannot be blamed for this type of behavior however, it is beyond their understanding. They simply cannot remember what is sinking to the bottom of their tank. May we ourselves never grow so busy and sleep deprived that we find ourselves in a similar circumstance!

By now I am sure many of you are screaming, *"What can we do to save our little fishy friends from this unfortunate dilemma?"* First of all, calm yourselves and stop screaming. People may begin to wonder if you've had enough sleep yourself. I think it is important to note that not all of our little underwater friends suffer this fate. If proper precautions are taken we can help these little boogers get some shut-eye (without shutting their eyes of course). Some of these methods are quite simple; others may take quite a bit of self-control on your part.

First, if you are a fish owner and have your own tank with happy little critters in it, control yourself. Do not run up to it, and flick on the light switch filling their world with blazing light, and then stick your shockingly large and possibly disturbing face up against the glass. This will only distress the fish further. Using a timer to activate the lights at regular intervals, and glancing at them from a safe distance is a good place to start.

Secondly, if you simply love to admire these creatures of splendor, do just that, admire them. Do not pound at rim of their world like a hungry ogre who is choosing his meal. Let us not forget, we do eat their family members, and I am sure this irony is disturbing enough to our scaly friends. I can only imagine the chaos that plagues them both day and night.

G: *"When do you think The-Dry-Ones will return Bob?"*
B: *"I'm not sure Gertrude, let's just try and get some sleep!"*
G: *"I can't sleep when I know that any minute my own bedroom will be flooded with light and one of Them will stare at me with their gigantic eyes that never stop staring, looking, always blinking…"*

B: *"Gertrude, you're losing it, stop thinking about The-Dry-Ones, you'll go up the shallow end!"*
G: *"I think I hear one coming Bob!"*
B: *"Oh no, it's the smaller one! Brace yourself!"*

POUND, POUND, POUND

Alas, another sleepless night for George and Gertrude. Shame on us! So care for your fish, approach them as you would a timid deer or sasquatch. They are tiny compared to you. They can see you and have only heard rumors of what the giant humans do to fish like them. Let us prove those rumors wrong.

Love them.

Speak quietly to them.

Respect their privacy.

In time, I believe that we will find happier and more content fish that are more rested and ready to face the day. They may even grow accustom to their owner and show more dazzling colors while bathing happily to the praise of their proud owner. Take a stand for the future of fish and human coexistence today. Finally, at the risk of sounding cliché, ***"Please don't tap on the glass!"***

So I Have This Theory...

Chapter 14
Manhood Choices

Ah manhood... that wonderful adventure which every young lad undertakes in becoming a man. A fantastic journey, filled with all kinds of adventure, uncertainty, fear, passion, pain, and decisions where both success and failure seem to be lurking around each and every corner. This quest has been known to take the smallest and scrawniest of boys and transform them into the world's strongest and most influential leaders. Every boy desires to know if he has what it takes to reach this goal of true manhood, and every man, once he has arrived, wishes he could return to his glorious boyhood years of bliss.

> What is it that makes this escapade into manhood such a meaningful and memorable process?
>
> Is it the adventures he faces along the journey, or the uncertainties of the future that awaits him?
>
> Perhaps it is the memories he makes along the way, or is it simply the plain excitement of being a guy?
>
> Could it be all of these mixed into a boyhood full of toy trains, army men, cars, and girls?

Might it consist of the mysteries of firecrackers, prom dates, or first drinks?

I would challenge you to look past all of these surface reasons and dig down a bit deeper in order to find the real truth behind this infamous voyage into manhood. To help you understand a bit more of a young man's perilous journey, I will ask you a few simple questions.

First off, how can a boy spend hours and hours setting up his wee little army men or multi-colored building blocks only to knock them all down or throw them back into the box simply because of lunchtime?

Why does a young man spend weeks reading car magazines and consumer reports only to test-drive dozens of cars before he chooses the perfect car for himself?

Why does a teenage guy fall madly in love with "the most beautiful girl in the world" only to discover a week later that her best friend just so happens to be "the woman of his dreams"?

Do any of these sound familiar?

"So Bobby, what do you want to be when you grow up?"
"What university are you going to attend Richard?"
"Hey Jack; have you found a job yet?"
"Honey, will you buy me a puppy?"
"Do you guys want pepperoni or sausage?"
"Do I look fat in this dress?"

Are you beginning to see the repeating trend? The answer is "choices" my friend. Boys are constantly bombarded with choices every single day as they grow into manhood. Not a single day passes in a young man's life without a barrage of choices thrown in his direction. Choices of all kinds, shapes, and sizes.

What should I eat?
How should I dress?
Who should I hang out with?
Which girl should I try to impress?
What job should I have?
Does my breath smell?
Did I put deodorant on this morning?
What is that smell, and is it me?

Endless volleys of choices and questions pound against a young man on his journey into manhood. How he answers these questions and if he chooses wisely will determine if he has what it takes or not. The choices are simple at times such as, "strawberry or grape jelly?" and much harder at other times, "will you marry me?" The adventure and the excitement lies in the choices and decisions the young man makes along his journey.

Now that I have your intrigued, try this one on for size. How does a young man make the right decision if he is not faced with the proper choice first?

Are we allowing boys to fully develop into the men they need to be if there are certain choices they are not even aware exist? In other words, what if there are choices out there that boys and young men are not making simply because they are not aware of them.

"Big deal Zwar," you might say, or *"They have enough choices as it is."* Both of these statements are very true, however, could it be that all the other choices are covering up the "big deal" choice that they truly need to make? What if there was a choice that had to be made at a young age in order for it to take affect later in life?

What a shame this would be if a young man were not made aware of this choice until it was too late. What if this choice so altered a young man's future that it literally changed his physical and mental capabilities later in life? This type of choice would almost be criminal to be kept a secret.

As you may have guessed by now, there most certainly is a choice such as this, and it is most definitely a life altering choice as well. Even more shocking is the fact that this choice has been somewhat of a mystery until quite recently, and it is my duty to unveil it to you today. So, just what is this amazing choice that every young gentleman should be aware? You need wait not a second longer.

> **Belly Theory:**
> **A man's belly grows to fit its natural surroundings. Thus, how a boy chooses to wear his pants, at a young age, determines his belly shape later in life.**

First, I would like to begin by giving credit where it is due. The theory I am about to impart on you may never have occurred to me if it were not for my three good friends and roommates who battled through these thoughts and shared their various opinions and experiences on this very subject. With the help of these men, as well as many others, I am very confident not only in the validity of this theory but also in the benefits of properly understanding its full implications. Thus, if you disagree with various parts of this priceless knowledge, or choose to disregard it completely, know that you are joining a swiftly dwindling minority.

I hate to be the one to break this to you, but the honest truth is that everyone is going to get a little extra tummy someday so you might as well enjoy it.

Now, before you get all huffy and throw this book across the room or call me any more names, let me tell you that if you are uncomfortable with this idea there are plenty of alternatives.

Believe it or not, you do not need to get a flabby tummy! You may call it whatever you wish, a healthy gut, a big belly, a round midsection, a roly-poly, a breadbasket, a spare tire, love handles, or even mini-me. The choice is still completely up to you!

I am sure that I need not mention we are the only species that voluntarily starves itself every now and then simply because it makes us feel better about ourselves. Try and make sense of that. We own refrigerators full of food, as well as overflowing pantries, yet choose to go around all day listening to our stomachs growl in their protest against our new low carb, low sugar diet.

I also feel the need to tell you that my **Belly Theory** is only fully accurate when referring to male individuals. This is not to say that under certain circumstances it does not also hold true with females as well. However, I believe that you will agree that in terms of consistency, men are better candidates for this type of phenomenon. Getting back to the most important of all manhood choices, we must first describe some terms, as well as establish a good visual representation so that we are all on the same page.

For most men there exist only two belly shapes. The "Hang Over Belt Slouch (HOB-S)" and the "Pulled Up Trouser Pooch (PUT-P)". Both have the capability of becoming great works of art that any man can successfully grow, maintain, and be very proud to display.

My theory also states that at a young age, a boy must choose which type of belly he wishes to grow into, and must wear his pants accordingly in order to shape and mold it into the type in which he so wishes. Below are visual representations of the HOB-S and PUT-P types of bellies.

HOB-S: Hang Over Belt Slouch

HOB-S: This type is best grown by first establishing the proper height at which the subject chooses his hang over to begin. This must be established at a young age as the length of pant will increase or decrease due to the adjusted height required. It is important to familiarize oneself with the regular use of a fine quality belt, as this is an important necessity to ensure the prevention of slippage that can occur on a day-to-day basis.

To properly care for this type of belly not much is needed. Simply nurture the belly through the growing process. Abstain from jiggling or slapping the belly and you will ensure a happy and healthy HOB-S belly in no time at all. A slight slouch or slump when sitting has been known to assist proper growth with this type of belly and can minimize its development time significantly.

PUT-P: Pulled Up Trouser Pouch

PUT-P: The first step in establishing this type of belly is to start with the proper wardrobe. Slightly large or loosely fitting pants are required for a PUT-P belly. This type of tummy is grown first by pulling the trousers up over the belly completely and then positioning the top of the pant near the naval area. A belt is not a necessary item when this type of belly is desired. At first, a subject may feel that his efforts are all in vain. Rest assured that this type of belly is a slow but worthwhile investment.

Proper care for the PUT-P type requires a fairly steady diet, as well as a proper understanding of the PUT-P attitude. If one chooses to successfully establish a proper PUT-P belly, then he must first understand that a relaxed and nonchalant view must be taken on life itself. He must learn to lean back when he walks, as well as sits. A slow commanding walk accompanied by head nods and large t-shirts may assist the PUT-P individual to fully appreciate his wonderfully established belly.

Utterly amazing eh? How can this possibly be missing from fourth grade science class, gym class, or locker room gossip? Now, I already hear you muttering, *"What could possibly be the benefits of being able to choose what belly shape you will have when you are older?"* Are you kidding me? Why pick chocolate over vanilla? Why care if you wear blue jeans or khakis? Why choose sandals over cowboy boots? The answer is ridiculously obvious. We get a choice!

We as humans love choices; we simply can't get enough of them. Not to mention that we are absolutely obsessed with trying to control the way we look, feel, or appear. Perhaps we know someone who has certain fashions or styles and we would like to acquire some of that pizzazz! Whatever the reason, if we can have the choice, we definitely want to know about it.

Let us look at a few individuals in history and compare their choice of belly types and see how it made them who they are today. Some of these men could be your role models or long-standing heroes due to their choice of belly shapes.

Popular PUT-P bellies can be found on such men as Napoleon Bonaparte, George Washington, Curly Howard, and Fred Mertz. This is quite an impressive list, but definitely not the only influential men who have chosen the very dignified PUT-P belly shape.

A list of no less important HOB-S bellies can be found on Winston Churchill, John Candy, Chris Farley, and Homer Simpson.

Again, all of these gentlemen have chosen to represent the HOB-S type belly and have worn it with dignity and pride! ***Well done men, I salute you!***

Fantastic, is it not? Young men now have the chance to choose what types of bellies they will be blessed with when they are older. With this simple knowledge they may also enjoy the happiness that can only come from a well formed and superbly nurtured tummy. There is no need to thank me dear friends. It is my pleasure to impart this knowledge upon you with the hope that you too will bless others with it someday.

Perhaps they too can learn to love and care for their tummies as they grow into living art forms of pride and personal accomplishment.

So I Have This Theory...

Chapter 15
Little Green Men

Ok, now I know what you are thinking; *"C'mon Zwar, everyone has a theory on aliens!"* I am quite aware of that my fine reader, but before you refer me back to my own **Originality Theory**, you should know that my theory on aliens has nothing to do with government cover-ups or green men from Mars. In fact, this ridiculous theory might even frighten those of you who think that aliens are merely the stuff of science fiction.

If you are the type who is unafraid of stepping out into the unknown, this may prove to be your favorite theory yet.

Be warned however, this theory may change the way you feel about yourself and your future, so unless you do not feel up to the task of facing the cold hard truth about yourself, please do not continue.

> **Alien Theory:**
> **Alien beings are merely evolved humans from our future. They are simply our progressed offspring after many generations of adaptation and development.**

Now, before you sign me up for a lovely padded room in the nutty house, allow me to explain this nugget of knowledge further. First, I think that this theory is one of my personal favorites for two reasons. One, I have always been fascinated with the idea of aliens and UFOs. And two, it allows me to poke fun at evolution and its fundamental weaknesses.

To establish my credibility on this subject, I did some quite extensive research of alien sightings and encounters. Even after I exhausted all of my reputable sources, like Wikipedia and YouTube, I found a few tidbits of valuable information in some magazines I picked up in the grocery check out line as well. All in all, I feel that the information I am about to impart upon you is both reputable and trustworthy.

So, let's get started by discussing all of the sightings and encounters we humans have had with these visitors from "other" planets. I would first like to discuss the startling similarities I found in the accounts given by people who claimed to have actually seen real aliens. I have shortened the full accounts because I know you have about as much patience as a puppy with a full bladder. Here are a few of the accounts:

"...it had long green arms and long green fingers..."

"...staring with large shiny eyes... moved its huge oval shaped head..."

"...stood about four feet tall... short legs and long arms..."

"...swayed on thin legs... a short torso..."

"...with its small mouth and large eyes..."

Sounds a little creepy, I will admit, but once you understand the truth behind aliens, I think that you will find it more endearing than creepy. So, if we continue with the evolution idea, how does this fit in with our witness accounts? Well, let's take a closer look at their accounts to see what we can piece together so far. The witnesses described long arms and fingers, large eyes and noggins, short legs, and an overall greenish tint. Doesn't really sound like a fine specimen of nature, but hey, I'm sure that's what the apes would have said about us right?

Why would humans change into these small, green, gangly, big-headed creatures? Wouldn't we get stronger, bigger, and better looking? I mean that is what evolution is supposed to do, right, make us cooler generation by generation? Well, I don't mean to burst your bubble my friend, but that's not the way evolution works.

First of all, evolution is merely adaptation to ones surroundings. Scientists believe that adaptation, over a long period of time, leads to permanent physical changes. So, if we apply the current surroundings that you and I are experiencing right now, and what we will be facing in the next few thousand years, it makes complete sense!

Still not comprehending my phenomenal babblings? Oh, my small minded reader, allow me to explain. Think about your current daily routine.

You get up, hike six miles to where the animals can be found, hunt down the weak ones, and then attack them with spears and rocks you collected the day before. After your kill, you cut up the meat, and drag it back to your cave to share with your tribe. Lastly, you cook the meat over the campfire you make with your bare hands... What? That's not what you did yesterday?

Of course it's not; that's because we have evolved to that point already, and we have passed that point as well. No longer do we need strength, endurance, and tough skin. Now, our days consist of waking up to pre-programmed coffee pots, blue toothed cell phone conversations, and two hour commutes in air-conditioned automobiles. Not to mention, climate controlled offices, freeze dried dinners, and late night comedy hours on plasma screened surround sound brilliance. No my friend, our bodies are completely un-adapted to thrive in our current form of lifestyle. You know what might help with this current type of lifestyle?

Maybe *longer arms* so that we could reach more from our office chair or couch cushion. (That would be really handy!)

I know what I could really use, *larger eyes*. That way I could watch T.V. from farther away, while still being able to look at my wife while she is talking to me. (That would save a few arguments!)

I know that I could text and type faster if I had *smaller fingers,* and I know that I would fit better in my compact car if I didn't have such long legs.

Something else that would be nice is to be able to remember more. I am always forgetting important information like passwords, cell numbers, websites, pin numbers, cheat codes... Maybe if I just had a *bigger head* to store it all, then I could remember the really important things in life.

I hope you see where I am going here my friend. Basically, if we continue down the road that we are currently on, we are going to have to adapt. **Our current bodies are adapted for too much physical activity.**

Oh sure, they are great for running, hunting, standing, being outside... but come on, who does any of that? What we need is a change. A physical change that will help us to function better in this world of high speed, high stress, and workaholism!

If we go along with the idea of evolution, where our bodies simply adapt to function better in our surrounding environments, then we must expect that after a few dozen generations we will begin to see some changes. We may begin to develop longer arms and fingers to allow us to multitask better. Then, we will need larger eyes in order to take in multiple screens of data and images, and of course we will need larger heads to store all of this critical information.

I suppose the parts that we do not use will simply wither away. So, as we advance as a human species, things like legs or muscles may become a thing of the past simply because we don't use them. Finally, since we do not need to go outdoors in the future, our skin will most definitely not need to maintain its pigment to protect us from the sun. We may even develop skin that can gain energy from LCD flat screens and computer monitors. Wouldn't that be neat!

So what do I believe we will look like in the future? Simple. We will be small, greenish men and women with large eyes and heads.

We will naturally develop long, thin arms and fingers and our legs and muscles will wither because we won't need them anymore. See my friend, it's simply science. One day, we will look back at the silly bodies you and I are using right now and chuckle with the novelty of our past selves.

This brings up an interesting point. Think back to the last time you went to the zoo. I'm sure you gawked at the lions and the zebras; probably walked past the penguins and polar bears, as well. Then, you arrived at the monkey cages. I'm sure you watched them swinging from their fake little trees doing disgusting things with their other monkey friends. You may have even chuckled to yourself as you thought, *"Wow, we have come such a long way as a species! Look at how dumb we used to be!"*

What if our future green selves want to do the same thing? Do you think that there will be little zoos in the future where undeveloped humans run around in their little cubicles and tiny, little green men and women watch them and chuckle to themselves at the stupidity of it all? I think that they will find something even better my friend. I think that they will simply come and view us in our own time.

Think about it; let's say that instead of going to the zoo to see the monkeys, you could actually check them out in their own habitat way before they evolved into humans. Wouldn't that be something? *"But Zwar, there is no way anyone can do that; you would have to go back in time to see ape-men before they evolved..."* Precisely, my friend!

Time travel sounds so insane to us, so impossible. But, imagine if you tried explaining how a Ford Focus works to a caveman back in the day. He would also think you were insane and probably try to club you.

I think that time travel is a simple thing for a race of super developed green humans to accomplish. So what would we do if we could time travel? We would probably do quite a few things, including going to the zoo.

To clarify, I would like to go back to all of the interviews of the "alien" sightings. Why on earth would there be little green men in our time, if we hadn't evolved into them yet? Could it be that they were merely bored on a weekend, and decided to take the family on a trip back in time to check out the funny old humans. Why do you suppose that we have never gotten to hang out with an "alien" or gotten a great picture with one? Why, if they are our future generations, are they being so mysterious about themselves?

Well, have you ever tried to explain to an ape at the zoo that you are really his distant cousin? No, you just stared at him with your large beady eyes, didn't you? Maybe we will only communicate with our minds in the future, and they cannot talk to us. Perhaps, our future selves know that we would freak out as a human race and alter the future and space time continuum if we came in contact with ourselves from the future.

Whatever their reasoning is for remaining silent, I am simply glad that they are out there watching us at any time or any place. It gives one a comforting feeling doesn't it? Think about it.

No matter where you are or where you go, you may have your future descendants watching your every move and laughing to themselves about how incredibly disgusting and stupid they used to be. I don't know about you, but it gives me the warm fuzzies!

So, to wrap up this **Alien Theory**, when it comes to the little green men in our future, I think there is only one thing to say; Not to steal someone else's famous catch phrase, but *"change, yes we can!"*

So I Have This Theory...

The End...*or is it?*

So I Have This Theory...

Have an idea or theory of your own? Want an expert's opinion?
Please submit them to me here: CalebZwar@gmail.com

So I Have This Theory...

THEORY INDEX

Hair Migration Theory
Hair, like all biological entities, grows weary and tiresome over extended periods of time. In its desire for adequate rejuvenation and reprieve, it may choose to relocate itself to less prominent areas for extended periods of rest and solitude.

Time Perspective Theory
The passage of time is not a fixed or definite amount. It varies due to the dimension or perspective in which it is experienced. Speed is relative to the amount of time one has experienced.

Cold Weather Theory
Exposing the human body to prolonged periods of cold temperatures, not only has adverse short-term effects on the body, but can also create long-term, physical and mental damages as well.

Originality Theory
We as a human race have grown lazy in the creation and discovery of new ideas and thoughts. We have grown accustom to re-making old ideas and are in danger of losing our creative and artistic abilities all together.

Yawn Theory
The triggering mechanism that results in the familiar stretching of the oral cavity known as yawning, originates in the ocular cavity. This common stretching exercise has multiple side effects, the most important of which is the lubrication of the vision sensory devices.

Human Order Theory
We as humans have cultivated and established a list of rules and guidelines by which we hold ourselves in restraint, and have come to fear what is outside of these boundaries. Only through breaking these regulations can we begin to expose and overcome them.

Mosquito Theory
The mosquito has used our sympathy for life to trick us into believing a lie. Mosquitoes, which are popular for their constant desire to drain us of our blood, do not actually require blood to survive.

Ancient Theory
In the year 2450 B.C. certain events occurred which formed the world into what we know it as today. These events are all related, and their connections answer many of the mysteries of the ancient world we once thought unexplainable.

Disgustingly Sanitary Theory
Humans that are concerned with sanitary cleanliness have a tendency to perform certain tasks out of habit or ignorance which they believe are aiding them in maintaining a pristine environment. However, many of these tasks are attaining quite opposite results.

Stuffy Nose Theory
Our noses become stuffy when we subject them to prolonged periods of tightly packed air. This blockage is relieved only when we increase the temperature of the particles, allowing them to depressurize and move freely.

Dragon Theory
In the Dark Ages, medieval knights and villagers killed off the remaining helpless dinosaurs simply out of fear and confusion then created stories of dragons and fire-breathing monsters.

Brain Freeze Theory
When a cold substance is introduced to the throat and esophagus, it causes the constriction of blood flow to the brain. Proper precautions can be taken to eliminate these effects all together.

Fish Theory

Fish do not sleep as we do; they catch short naps between their darting movements. These delicate sleep patterns, if compromised, can have terrible repercussions on their energy levels, memory capacities, and thought processes.

Belly Theory

A man's belly grows to fit its natural surroundings. Thus, how a boy chooses to wear his pants, at a young age, determines his belly shape later in life.

Alien Theory

Alien beings are merely evolved humans from our future. They are simply our progressed offspring after many generations of adaptation and development.

Sources

Pg #78

"may" Merriam-Webster.com. Merriam-Webster, 2011. Web. 6 Oct. 2011.

"I" Merriam-Webster.com. Merriam-Webster, 2011. Web. 6 Oct. 2011.

"take" Merriam-Webster.com. Merriam-Webster, 2011. Web. 6 Oct. 2011.

"your" Merriam-Webster.com. Merriam-Webster, 2011. Web. 6 Oct. 2011.

"order" Merriam-Webster.com. Merriam-Webster, 2011. Web. 6 Oct. 2011.

Pg #148

"dragon" Merriam-Webster.com. Merriam-Webster, 2009. Web. 23 Aug. 2009.

"dragon" OxfordDictionaries.com. Oxford, 2009. Web. 23 Aug. 2009.